THE FINAL CUT

Frederick Van Veen

Contents

Introduction

In 2006 I began writing a blog under the pretentious title *The Literary Beachcomber*. I did read a lot; thus the "literary" part. The "beachcomber" part was easy. I live on a beautiful beach in Maine, and I like to walk the sands and pick up whatever the tide washes in.

Soon I had written enough blogs to publish a book's worth of them. The first blog book was called *Searching for Joan Leslie*. If you are as old as I am, you may remember Joan as a movie actress in the 1940s.

Having learned how to do it, I wrote a few other blog books. The blogs were about movies, politics, the Maine weather, growing up in Dorchester, etc,

This is a collection of blogs about the arts, or at least those arts that interest me. The title reflects the fact that this is likely to be the final book in the series. I owe thanks to my son Chris, who contributed the title, cover photo, and design, and my daughter, Amy Palmer, who proofread and edited the text.

Frederick Van Veen
January, 2014

Anthony Trollope

Y ou don't have to be retired to tackle Trollope's "Barsetshire" and "Palliser" novels, but it helps. Each series is spread over six densely packed novels, and my 12 volumes contain more than 8000 pages of golden prose.

It's not as bad as it sounds. If you attack the Pallisers first, saving the Barsetshire series for another day, you whittle the exercise down to about 4000 pages, which, at 200 pages a week, will take you only 20 weeks to read.

The larger question is, why embark on such a long voyage in the first place?

Well, as any number of Trollope loyalists will tell you, the stories are fascinating, the writing flawless, and you will learn much about life in mid-nineteenth-century England. The Palliser series is about politics, which at the time was the realm of maneuver, backbiting, blackmail, and character assassination. (Today's American reader will feel right at home.) The central character is Plantagenet Palliser, known by his friends as Planty Pal, an earnest, wellborn MP who rises through the government ranks on the strength of talent, attention to detail, and an ability to stay apart from most of the nastier battles. He is a good man, but his wife, Glencora, is flighty in the extreme, and her escapades, some with an old flame who won't quit, are a source of continued embarrassment to her husband.

Dozens of interesting people weave their ways through the six novels, none more fascinating than the title character in *Lady Eustace's Diamonds*. Lizzie Greystock marries up and becomes Lady Eustace, and a year later she is a wealthy widow. There follows a titanic confrontation between Lady Eustace and her late husband's family over a valuable diamond necklace. The contest turns on an interesting English legalism: Lady Eustace claims that the diamonds were a gift from her husband and are thus rightfully hers. The family contends that the diamonds have been theirs for generations and are thus classified as an heirloom, belonging by rights to the family in perpetuity. It is the sort of dispute that keeps lawyers in business, and in this case it also keeps Lady Eustace in skullduggery – and allows Trollope to create a rogue's gallery of shifty characters.

The political winds that swirl about Planty Pal involve a move to convert the currency to the decimal system and a proposal to disestablish the Church of England (i.e., to deprive it of State support). Every schoolchild is taught at some point that "antidisestablishmentarianism" is the longest word in the English language, and now we know what it means.

The Barsetshire novels also deal with politics, but here it is the politics of the Church of England – which is also the realm of maneuver, backbiting, etc. One of the most memorable of all Trollope characters is the Rev. Obadiah Slope, chaplain to Bishop Proudie. Slope is ambitious, duplicitous, and, all in all, a rat. The Bishop is ineffective, and he dithers while his overbearing wife makes the major decisions. You can see the war clouds gathering as Slope and Mrs. Proudie circle each other, increasingly at odds over diocesan matters, and when the explosion comes it does not disappoint. Slope is one of Trollope's juiciest characters, and he and Mrs. Proudie demonstrate that Dickens wasn't the only writer with a gift for names.

The Palliser and Barsetshire novels were both filmed by the BBC some years ago, and both are available on DVD. In the former case, the entire series takes a dozen discs. It starts slowly, but overall it is creditable. Lady Glencora and Planty Pal are played by Susan Hampshire and Philip Latham, with supporting roles filled by actresses familiar to all Masterpiece Theater fans: Barbara Murray and Anna Massey.

The BBC's Barchester series is distinctly weaker. Most of it is based on *The Warden*, the first and the thinnest of the six volumes. Donald Pleasance is fine as the beleaguered warden, and Alan Rickman is perfect as Slope, but nine-tenths of the Barsetshire material is simply omitted, as if the producers ran out of money.

But what is grievously missing in both film versions is Trollope himself. One of the delights of these books is the occasional insertion of the author's comments – an aside, as if intended for your ears only. After reading a hundred pages or more about Lady Eustace, for instance, you will have decided that she is a thoroughly despicable person. But then along comes Trollope to say something like, "I know the reader will think ill of this person based on the circumstances in which I have placed her, but she really has many admirable qualities," which he will then enumerate. Such private communications from author to reader, over a distance of 150 years, undoubtedly help explain why so many people are so devoted to this writer.

Apart from the two series, Trollope wrote a number of other novels, including *He Knew He Was Right*, and *The Way We Live Now*, both given the full treatment by the BBC, with sterling scripts by Andrew Davies and first-class performances by Bill Nighy, David Suchet, Matthew Macfadyen, and others from the BBC's galaxy. You may want to sample one of these before taking the plunge. *The Way We Live Now*, with financial scams at its heart, will be familiar territory to an American audience. But if you can afford the time, dive into the first of the Palliser novels, *Can You Forgive Her?* I recommend it, and Anthony Trollope just told me I am right to do so.

Dawn Powell

In 1970, convicts from Riker's Island deposited an unclaimed female body in New York City's paupers' cemetery, Hart Island, where it joined many thousands of unidentified corpses fished out of the East River or found in New York's mean streets. The woman had died five years earlier, and her remains had been willed to the Cornell Medical Center. It was customary for the Center to return the body to the family when it was through with it. But no one wanted the body, and in 1970 the deceased's executor authorized the hospital to dispose of the remains "in the City cemetery."

The lady buried in Hart Island is one of my favorite authors, Dawn Powell. She wrote 15 novels, 10 plays, hundreds of short stories, and a diary covering more than 35 years. But in 1970, all her works were out of print, and no one knew about Dawn Powell.

Think of it: This writer, who had once been a prized member of a circle that included John Dos Passos, Ernest Hemingway, J.B. Priestly, John LaTouche, Malcolm Cowly, and other literary lions, died in total obscurity. How *sic transit* can you get?

Today, Powell has been rediscovered. More than ten of her novels have been reprinted, and when her diaries were published in 1995, one reviewer called it "one of the outstanding literary finds of the past quarter century." Gore Vidal was among those who declared that this long-forgotten lady of letters was one of the best writers this country has ever produced.

Dawn Powell was born in Ohio in 1896, the second of three daughters. Their mother died when Dawn was seven. The father remarried, and Dawn's stepmother was, by most accounts, abusive. At age 13, Dawn (who had even then decided she wanted to be a writer) fled her home and took refuge with an aunt. She eventually graduated from Lake Erie College in 1918 and then left Ohio for New York City, hoping to earn a living as a writer.

If this much has whetted your appetite, you can find out more about Powell in Tim Page's 1998 biography *Dawn Powell* (Henry Holt). My interest here lies in her writing.

Most of Powell's novels were set in New York, and several have been republished in recent years and have attracted a new following. These include *Angels on Toast, A Time to be Born*, and *The Wicked Pavilion*, which Edmund Wilson called "quite on a level with (the novels of) Anthony Powell, Evelyn Waugh and Muriel Spark." The best of these is *Angels on Toast*, which deals with a couple of wheeling and dealing businessmen, their wives and girlfriends.

Powell's New York novels are witty, but they are a bit edgy for my taste, and I much prefer the Ohio novels, particularly *Dance Night*, in which the folks in gritty, industrial Lamptown escape the depression blues every Thursday night by heading to the Casino Dance Hall. In a 1957 interview, Powell said that she thought it her best work. Her other Ohio novels were *She Walks in Beauty, The Bride's House* (Powell's first important novel), *The Tenth Moon*, and *The Story of a Country Boy*.

Then there is my personal favorite, *My Home is Far Away*. This is a fictionalized but obviously autobiographical account of the wretched upbringing she and her sisters endured at the hands of their stepmother and of their search for safety. It's a melancholy story, but the writing is anything but melancholy. In fact, it is positively lyrical.

Here is how it opens:

"This was the month of cherries and peaches, of green apples beyond the grape arbor, of little dandelion ghosts in the grass, of sour grass and four-leaf clovers, of still dry heat holding the smell of nasturtiums and dying lilacs. This was the best month of all and the best day. It was not birthday, Easter, Christmas, or picnic, but all these things and something else, something wonderful, something utterly unknown. The two little girls in embroidered white Sunday dresses knew no way to express their secret joy but by whirling each other dizzily over the lawn crying, 'We're moving! We're moving! We're moving to London Junction!'

The novel then spins the story of the Willard girls, Lena, Marcia (i.e., Dawn), and Florrie, as they cope with the death of their mother and their father's marriage to the decidedly unmotherly Idah Hawkins. Idah, modeled on Powell's stepmother Sabra, is bad news, and the girls' world collapses around them.

This is where *Home* draws its strength. While I found the characters in Powell's New York novels interesting, I didn't really care what happened to them. But I cared about Marcia and her sisters, deeply, all the way through the novel. You will too, if you read it. No wonder the New York Times Book Review called the novel "one of the permanent masterpieces of childhood."

The book was first published in 1944, and it was republished in paperback a few years ago. In their original printings, none of Dawn Powell's books earned even a second edition. The latest edition of *My Home is Far Away* is now in its fourth printing.

Dawn Powell's biography, letters, and diaries describe an incredibly talented lady, whom fate treated badly. The opening and closing chapters of her life were especially difficult. She had her moments of triumph in middle age, but they were fewer than she deserved. Her remains are still in Hart Island, as far as I know. But her books are now alive and thriving again, and that's probably what she would have wanted most.

Nevil Shute

I can hear, telepathically, many readers saying, "I don't have the time for Trollope, or the inclination for Waugh." I just want a good story told without the frills, a quick and easy read that I can take with me on a flight from BOS to LAX." I have just the writer for you. His name is Nevil Shute.

Shute, whose real name was Nevil Shute Norway, is best known for his novel *On the Beach*, a somber tale of nuclear Armageddon, made into a memorable film starring Gregory Peck. But *On the Beach* is not at all like Shute's 20-plus other novels, which are mostly uplifting stories about ordinary people doing extraordinary things in interesting settings. Shute's personal history (aeronautical engineer, inventor, war correspondent, adventurer) comes through in his writing, but the real attraction is his knack of dreaming up good stories and telling them well.

Take, for instance, *Pied Piper*. John Howard, a stodgy British bachelor, is on a fishing holiday in Switzerland on the eve of the Second World War. Friends in Zurich, afraid that the Germans might not honor their country's neutrality, beg Howard to take their two young children with him on his return to London. He agrees, and the trio sets off on a westward overland journey through France, just a step ahead of the Germans all the way. At various points, French parents implore Howard to add their small children to the troupe. Howard, who is not that fond of

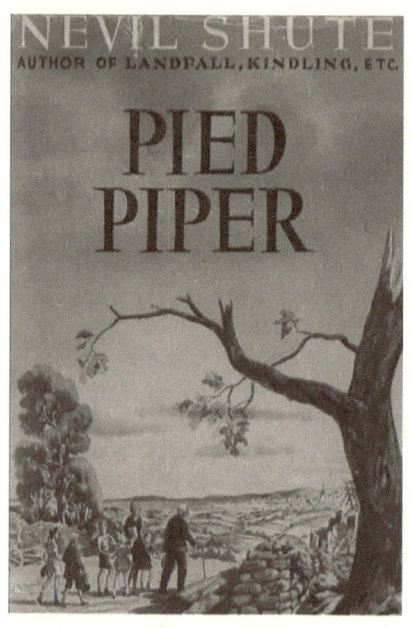

children, thus becomes a pied piper. In the final chapters, in which Howard and his charges are captured by the Germans just short of the Channel and safety, Shute concocts an ingenious but credible plot resolution.

Trustee From the Tool Room takes place just after the war, when Britain, facing a financial crisis, imposes harsh currency controls. A British yachtsman converts his considerable wealth into gold bars, which he then conceals in the hull of his boat. He then sets sail for the South Pacific with his wife, leaving his small daughter with a friend until he is resettled on the other side of the globe. Months pass, and then word reaches London that the sailboat foundered on a reef in a remote part of French Polynesia. The friend alone knows of the treasure buried in the hull (an expert machinist, he had helped conceal the gold) – treasure that rightfully belongs to the little girl in his care. He cannot reveal the truth about the illegally transported gold, of course, so the task of getting to the Pacific and salvaging the hoard is his alone. He is another of Shute's ordinary people in an extraordinary situation.

The Far Country tells of the attempts of a young Eastern European doctor to forge a new, post-war life in Australia, the complications that arise when he is exposed as an ex-member of the Wehrmacht, and the romance that develops when an English girl visits. It's a good read and an interesting window on life in small-town Australia.

No Highway will appeal to engineers. The hero, an expert in metal fatigue employed by a British aircraft maker, is convinced that the tail section of a new passenger plane is structurally flawed. The plane has just entered service, big money is on the line, and the engineer's dire prediction is ridiculed – partly because he is also known to be a bit of a religious flake. When he finds himself flying across the Atlantic on an airliner whose flying time has just hit what he believes to be its theoretical limit, the scene is very suspenseful. You feel sure that Shute will not let his hero die in mid-book, but then, the alternative is to discredit his theory. What happens? You'll have to read the book.

The best of all the Shutes is *The Legacy*, whose later editions were retitled *A Town Like Alice* after a popular 1981 Australian TV miniseries based on the book. The saga begins with the fall of Singapore and the forced march of a group of British women up the Malayan peninsula, follows one of the survivors (Jean Paget, our heroine) back to post-war London, returns to Malaya, and concludes with an odyssey in Australia. It is all very moving, and in my view it is Shute's masterpiece. The

Australian miniseries does the book full justice. In fact, it is terrific. Unfortunately, a DVD version does not yet exist, but a VHS tape is available.

The film versions of Shute's other books are a mixed bag. *Pied Piper* was a 1942 movie starring Monty Woolley as John Howard. *The Far Country* was turned into a miniseries starring Michael York as the doctor. Neither of these is worth your time. Jimmy Stewart and Marlene Dietrich turned *No Highway* into an above average film. But none of these three films measures up to its book.

Most used-book stores have some Shutes on their shelves, and if you spot a copy of *Pied Piper* or *Trustee from the Tool Room*, grab it. Or look for Shute at your local library. Even our little library in Kennebunkport has a dozen or so of his titles on hand. Chances are that once you polish off one of Nevil Shute's novels, you'll be looking for others.

Evelyn Waugh Revisited

I just finished Julian Fellowes's first novel, *Snobs*, and it leaves me with the feeling that Evelyn Waugh is alive and well and writing under the name Julian Fellowes. Fellowes made a career of acting in pedestrian British TV series until the late nineties, when, at age 50-plus, he decided to turn it on. First came a lucky break: Robert Altman signed him on to write the screenplay for *Gosford Park*. That brought an Academy Award for best original screenplay. Bingo. Then a juicy role in the popular BBC series, *Monarch of the Glen*, then his first stint as a film director (as well as screenwriter) for *Separate Lies*, a fine movie starring Tom Wilkinson, Emily Watson, and Rupert Everett. And now the novel, published by St. Martin's Press. According to the book jacket, he has also written the book for a Cameron Macintosh musical based on *Mary Poppins*. How he finds time to do all this is a mystery. Having witnessed his acting, writing, and directing achievements, I can say that it is all quality work.

Snobs concerns the campaign of a London beauty, Edith Lavery, to invade the upper ranks of British society by snagging Charles Broughton, a certified earl who oversees a huge estate, Broughton Hall. Yes, Edith Wharton has already covered that ground, but this is today, not yesterday, and the moral landscape has changed, at least for the world around the Broughtons. Edith captures her man, to the horror of his family, and in short order finds that the life she coveted is a crashing bore. A film crew obtains permission from the Broughtons to use the estate for a shoot, and this brings Edith into contact with a handsome actor who seems to offer her an escape. To tell you more would be wrong, although the appeal of the book lies, not in its plot, but in its observations on the British class system. And here is where Fellowes becomes Waugh. Samples: "The English, of all classes as it happens, are addicted to exclusivity. Leave three Englishmen in a room and they will invent a rule that prevents a fourth joining them."

Or this: "To the English skin is, as rule, the compliment of last resort, to be employed when there is nothing else to praise. Good skin is frequently dwelt on when talking of the plainer members of the royal family."

Of course, one book does not make an ouvre, and Waugh's place in the pantheon is secure. Still, off this first effort, one hopes that Fellowes has enough ammunition left over to reload and fire off a few more salvos. He is a man of genuine talent.

(After this blog was originally published, Fellowes wrote the miniseries Downton Abbey, a blockbuster success.)

Waugh and Greene: The Masters

In terms of shelf space in my library, Evelyn Waugh is second only to E.F. Benson (about whom more, much more, later), and Graham Greene certainly ranks in the top five.

Many people regard Evelyn Waugh the best English-language writer of the twentieth century. If there is a complaint, it is that his writing is so stylish that, for me at least, it sometimes gets in the way of the story. I find myself marveling at his composition of a paragraph instead of considering how the paragraph advances the story he is telling. No one handled the language as skillfully as Waugh, over such a span of years.

The comparison with Greene is inevitable because they were both converts to Catholicism and both used their adopted religion as a fulcrum for many of their stories. Many of Waugh's contemporaries found his use of religious conflict off-putting, but in most of Greene's stories morality and not religion dominated, and he was more likely to be known (as he desired) as a writer who happened to be Catholic than as a Catholic writer.

Greene was by far the better story-teller of the two, and for this reason his novels were much easier to translate to the screen than Waugh's. Greene's *The Third Man* is one of the true screen classics of all time, and his *Our Man in Havana*, *The Quiet American* (the remake, starring Michael Caine), and *The Power and the Glory* are all excellent movies. A Jesuit, Gene Phillips, has written a perceptive analysis of the Greene films, (*Graham Greene: The Films of his Fiction*), and it is recommended for anyone who is seriously into movies.

When I was in high school, two of Greene's more interesting novels were published: *The Heart of the Matter* and *The End of the Affair*. I read both at the time and enjoyed them. The plots are heavily religious (more like what you'd expect from Waugh). *Matter* is about Scobie, a police official in British Africa, who is torn between his affection for a German girl washed ashore after her ship is torpedoed and his marriage vows to a dull wife who is eager to move to a more civilized place. What takes this out of the ordinary is the effect of his Catholicism on the devout Scobie. *The End of the Affair* covers similar ground: A married woman and her lover are caught in a London air raid, a bomb explodes in their trysting place, and she fears that Bendrix, her lover, has been killed. The woman, Sarah, promises God that if He spares Bendrix she will give him up. He does, and she does, confounding her agnostic lover.

Both *Matter* and *Affair* were made into movies, and the results were disappointing. Miscasting (Van Johnson as Bendrix) didn't help, and Trevor Howard's solid portrayal of Scobie couldn't overcome the dark look of *Matter*. Also, the prevailing morality code dictated that the movie version not end with a suicide (as the book does), and the revised ending was utterly implausible.

One of Greene's best novels, turned into a riveting movie by Greene the screenwriter, is *The Comedians*. This is a powerful story about life in Haiti under the tyrant Papa Doc Duvalier, written and filmed while Duvalier was in power. (Haiti was off-limits for the film crew, needless to say, and Haiti was recreated in Africa.) The cast could hardly be better: Richard Burton, Alec Guinness, Peter Ustinov, and Elizabeth Taylor, all in top form. The story itself is chilling and unforgettable. If you haven't seen it, by all means do. There is no better example of the artistry of Graham Greene, both as a story-teller and a scenarist.

Waugh is another matter. Stripped of his luminous writing style, Waugh's stories as stories do not translate well to the screen, with one glowing exception. *Brideshead Revisited*, his masterpiece, was made into a miniseries in England, and in my view it towers above anything seen on television before or since. It is simply exquisite, thanks to John Mortimer's meticulously faithful screenplay, which manages to preserve most of what makes *Brideshead* such a great read.

Otherwise, Waugh falls flat on film. *Handful of Dust* is a good book, a dull movie. *The Loved One*, a delicious black comedy about the mortuary scene in Hollywood, was turned into a grotesque film. *Scoop*, a funny novel about the writer of a newspaper gardening column who, through a bureaucratic mix-up, is assigned to cover an imminent war in Africa, was well done by British TV in 1987, but the film, which I managed to see, was given no exposure in the U.S. *Black Mischief* would be too politically incorrect to be attempted today, though the story, centering on the attempts of a British-educated black man to bring his African country into the twentieth century, is absolutely hilarious and worth reading.

Vile Bodies, Waugh's breakthrough novel, is all style and little substance, and poor movie material. (This novel, more than any other, serves as the prototype for Julian Fellowes's *Snobs*, discussed in an earlier blog.) But Waugh was not writing with Hollywood or Ealing in view, whereas Greene wrote most of his novels with the camera in mind – and in fact often wrote the screenplays based on his novels.

Their lives mirrored their art. Waugh lived his life in England in more or less conventional surroundings, with wives Evelyn (yes, Evelyn) and then Laura and children. Greene, on the other hand, abandoned England for the French Riviera and maintained various extra-marital liaisons until the end (one of these a long-running affair with a married American woman). Waugh became increasingly conservative and curmudgeonly in his old age, while Greene veered to the political left.

Both writers are treated exhaustively in numerous biographies, most of which sit in my library, as do Waugh's published letters and diaries. This essay is intended only for those who want a taste, not the whole banquet.

E.F. Benson

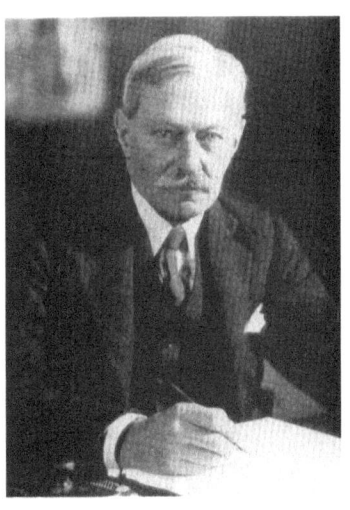

Whenever I visit a used-book store, I head first for the B's, to see if there is anything on the shelf by E.F. Benson. The search requires visits to the fiction and nonfiction sections, for Benson wrote both. His total output was well over 100 books, mostly novels but also biographies (of Queen Victoria, King Edward VII, Charlotte Bronte, Sir Francis Drake, and Ferdinand Magellan, among others), memoirs, collections of short stories, and plays. Today most of his books are out of print, and this adds zest to the quest. I have about 30 of his books now, and when I find a new one it is a cause for celebration.

E.F. Benson was born in 1867, the fifth of six children of the Archbishop of Canterbury. The first son, Martin, died at 17. Arthur (A.C.) became Master of Magdalen College, Cambridge. Two daughters, Nellie and Maggie, died young, the latter in an insane asylum. The youngest son, Hugh (R.H.) jolted his Anglican parents by converting to Catholicism and becoming a Catholic priest (ordained by the Pope, no less). Arthur and Hugh both became prolific writers. And then there was E.F., known as Fred, by far the most talented member of a talented family.

Those who recognize the name of E.F. Benson today almost certainly know him by his Lucia books, still available in paperback and in an omnibus edition. Lucia (full name: Emmeline Lucas) is one of the great comic creations of twentieth-century literature. Lucia's ambition is to be the unquestioned trendsetter in her community (usually Tilling), and to this end she assumes continental airs, drops errant *mots* ("au reservoir"), and relentlessly attempts to outmaneuver her chief rival, Elizabeth Mapp. The duels between these two, as deadly serious as any of Napoleon's campaigns, were the basis for a BBC television series called *Mapp and Lucia*.

Lucia is a hoot, and the Lucia books – *Queen Lucia, Lucia in London, Miss Mapp, Mapp and Lucia, The Male Impersonator, The Worshipful Lucia,* and *Trouble for Lucia* – are wonderfully funny. But there is much, much more to Benson than Lucia.

One of the funniest books I have ever read is Benson's *Secret Lives*. It is a laughing-out-loud read, and, best of all, it is still in print (a Hogarth Press paperback). When I say "funny" I don't mean Dave Barry funny or Saturday Night Live funny. I mean humor that arises when stuffy, pompous people are placed in comic, absurd situations, made even more absurd by the elegance of the prose.

The characters in *Secret Lives* are the residents of Durham Square, a small, private neighborhood in Edwardian London. Among these are the reigning doyenne Margaret Mantrip, writing a biography of her late father, a vicar who cleaned up the Square by driving out the scarlet women; Eva Lowndes, who sees halos over the heads of her friends, the colors of these halos revealing the characters of their owners; Elizabeth Conklin, with her 10 Pekinese dogs (the rotund lady, with her 10 leashes, is likened to a big balloon being borne along by the wind); the present vicar, a passionate believer in reincarnation; and the mysterious newcomer Susan Leg, who is immediately stamped as lowbrow by Ms. Mantrip. The chief secret of the book's title is the fact that Susan Leg is in reality Rudolph da Vinci, the author of the trashy best-selling novels devoured by Ms. Mantrip. Thus, as long ago as 1932, Benson was writing his own Da Vinci code.

Benson's first success as an author was an 1893 novel *Dodo*, in which the title character is a flighty English socialite. Then, over the next four decades, came an outpouring of books, fiction and nonfiction, spanning a wide range of interests. He was, for instance, a competitive ice skater, one of the best in England, and he wrote the definitive book on the subject (*English Figure Skating*). He was also an archeologist who wrote learned journal articles on digs in Greece and Egypt. His devotion to his family was on display in *Mother* and *Our Family Affairs*. His observations on Edwardian life and customs, in a volume called *As We Were*, won wide praise when it was published in 1930. But he is best known, and properly so, as one of the best comic novelists of his era.

Benson's last book was a memoir called *Final Edition*. He delivered it to his publisher just before he died, in 1940. He outlived all his siblings, and, since none of them ever married, his death marked the end of the line.

Considering his place in literary history and the memoirs written by him and by his brothers, surprisingly little is known about the private life of E.F. Benson. His biographers admit frustration in trying to delve into his motivations, his philosophy, his politics, and his personal relationships. Benson was able to explore his mother's life in detail in *Mother*, but such analysis was a one-way street. Once, when asked about her son, she simply said, "Fred's a sphinx." His was indeed a secret life.

Today, relatively few people are aware of the delights found in E.F. Benson's novels. But these few are a dedicated lot. Some keep the author's memory alive through the activities and publications of the Tilling Society, which, by the way, gives free life memberships to all applicants 100 years old or older.

Einstein's Dreams

Have you ever wondered about the nature of time? Of course you have. I have. We all have, including Einstein, who wondered about time a great deal and finally came to grips with it in 1905, when he published four remarkable treatises, including one setting out his theory of relativity.

The possibility of time travel has excited fiction-writers for many years, and even though I have seen *The Time Machine* often, I never tire of watching Weena and her simple-minded Eloi friends escape the Morlocks. Countless other time-travel tales engage us, even though we know the basic premise is impossible.

Or is it?

Last night I read a little book called *Einstein's Dreams*. It was written by an MIT professor named Alan Lightman, and it is one of those books you can't put down. The subject matter is the hook, but the fact that Lightman is a good writer is the grabber.

The book, in a mere 179 pages, explores the possibilities attached to various theories about the nature of time, some well known, some not so. Maybe time is a repetitive phenomenon. Maybe time does not exist outside our perception. Maybe, since time is related to mass, it passes more slowly the farther you are from the earth's core. Maybe there are two kinds of time:

mechanical time and body time. Maybe, because time passes more slowly for people in motion, those who travel at high speed gain time.

The book is organized as a series of vignettes, dated throughout 1905 and separated by "interludes" in which Einstein chats with his friend Besso in Berne. But Einstein's fantasies of various time-altered "worlds" are the attraction here, along with the metaphysical points they make. Take this picture of a world in which everyone travels at high velocity to gain time:

"A man or a woman suddenly thrust into this world would have to dodge houses and buildings. For all is in motion. Houses and apartments, mounted on wheels, go careening through Bahnhofplatz and race through the narrows of Marktgasse, their occupants shouting from second-floor windows. The post office doesn't remain on Postgasse, but flies through the city on rails, like a train. ….Everywhere the air whines and roars with the sound of motors and locomotion. When a person comes out of his front door at sunrise, he hits the ground running, catches up with his office building, hurries up and down flights of stairs, works at a desk propelled in circles, gallops home at the end of the day…..No one is still."

The book was widely praised when it was first published, but it took me a while to discover the small volume, which has been sitting in my library, unnoticed, for at least 10 years. What made me decide to pick it up last night? Why did Einstein have his "annus mirabilis" the same year my mother was born? Why did I choose to quote the paragraph above, only noting afterward that it was dated May 29, my birthday?

Tonight, still in my own private time warp, I read the short story "Germelshausen," by Friedrich Gerstäcker, which takes place in a small German village that comes to life for one day every hundred years. I remember reading it in German when I was in high school, but then I knew it as "Das Geheimnisvollen Dorf" (the full-of-mystery village). It's a lovely tale, used as the basis for *Brigadoon*. And further proof that, no matter how surely we are prisoners of mechanical time, the idea of breaking free of those chains is endlessly fascinating.

Anthony Powell

We've talked about several of the great British authors of the last century or two – Waugh, Greene, Trollope, and others – and now it is time to address Anthony Powell, a true titan, a master of the novelist's art – and a writer hardly known to the American public.

I was put onto Powell about 30 years ago, when at a financial conference in London I struck up a conversation with a British financial manager about – what else? – books. He told me, in a tone that reeked of triumphalism, that he had just finished reading Powell's *Dance to the Music of Time* – a second time!! The full impact of this feat hit me only when I learned that *Dance* is not a book but a series of 12 novels spanning the period from just after World War 1 through two decades beyond World War 2. That trail is well worn, but Powell's characters make it seem brand new.

Powell wrote the first novel in the series, *A Question of Upbringing*, in 1951, the twelfth, *Hearing Secret Harmonies*, in 1975. How many writers can labor on a single narrative for 24 years? Just keeping the characters straight is an achievement, especially as a character may enter in volume 3, exit in volume 4, and resurface in volume 11, by which time you may have forgotten all about him or her. I found this a problem as I worked my way through the 12 books, and I must also say that the best of the 12 are the first three or four and that the last few are the weakest. The series is nevertheless an impressive achievement and one of the literary landmarks of our time.

The novels begin by examining the friendship of four boys in an Eton-like school in the early twenties: the narrator, Nicholas Jenkins, and his friends Charles Stringham, Peter Templer, and, memorably, Kenneth Widmerpool. At the outset Widmerpool's cluelessly inane behavior seems to mark him as comic relief, but by the end of the series, the buffoon emerges as a darker, more threatening presence.

Powell (rhymes with pole, not with towel) lived a long, productive life, which ended in 2000 when he was 95. There were many other novels (his first was published in 1931), biographies, critical essays, and at least two plays. He was a contemporary of Waugh and Greene at Oxford. In World War 2 he worked for British Intelligence, and the three *Dance* volumes dealing with the War are widely regarded as among the best covering that period.

There is something about a novel series that is especially satisfying. Finish one good read, then greet many of the same characters again in a new book, and so on, until the whole tapestry is hung – at which point you feel either relief or loss, depending on the quality of the story. Some of Dickens's and Trollope's best works first appeared as serials in newspapers, with readers anxiously awaiting each new episode. The literary serial as a genre has morphed into today's miniseries.

Anthony Powell's *Dance to the Music of Time* was in fact produced as a television miniseries in England about 10 years ago. The cast included John Gielgud, Edward Fox, and Zoë Wanamaker. The 50-year span was compressed into four two-hour segments, and reports from abroad say it was superb. For now, we'll have to take their word for it; the series was never aired in the U.S., nor is it available in the standard (NTSC) format for American VCRs or DVDs. If you have a player that can handle the British format (PAL), you can probably find a tape or disc at Amazon or eBay.

Ethan Mordden on Musicals

As any reader of these posts knows by now, I have long been a follower of musical theater. I have seen most of the classics, many of them in their original Broadway incarnations. My shelves are crammed with original-cast CDs and LPs, videotapes, and DVDs. My heroes are Richard Rodgers, Irving Berlin, John Kander, Fred Ebb, Stephen Sondheim, George Gershwin, Jerome Kern, and their contemporaries who gave us so many wonderful memories. I have read their biographies. I play their songs on my piano.

I take my children to musicals every chance I get, and I rattle on about them when we are together. As a result, they probably think their dad knows more than anyone alive about musical theater. Sorry, kids, but a man named Ethan Mordden knows a hundred times as much about musicals as I do. What's more, he is a fine writer. If you have even a wisp of interest in the subject, I strongly recommend his series of books on Broadway musicals. The more familiar you are with the great and not-so-great shows, the more you will get out of the books, but even if you're only dimly aware of *South Pacific* and *The Sound of Music*, you'll enjoy the stories.

The six books in the series cover six decades, to wit:

Make Believe; The Broadway Musical in the 20s.
Sing for Your Supper: The Broadway Musical in the 30s.
Beautiful Mornin': The Broadway Musical in the 40s.
Coming Up Roses: The Broadway Musical in the 50s.
Open a New Window: The Broadway Musical in the 60s.
One More Kiss: The Broadway Musical in the 70s.

Many people believe that the golden age of the musical was the period from the 40s (*Oklahoma!, Carousel*) through the 60s (*Cabaret, My Fair Lady*), and the best of Mordden's work are the books covering those decades. As the century wound down, the musicals became less innovative, the music less melodic, the lyrics less clever, and Mordden skewers the musicals of the last 25 years in *The Happiest Corpse I've Ever Seen*. In this acerbic wrap-up, he doesn't mince words: Musicals, he laments, have been going downhill, for a variety of reasons. (If you doubt this, consider the number of revivals playing the Great White Way these days.)

Mordden's writing sparkles. Here, for instance, is an excerpt from his loving description of one of my favorites, the 1963 musical *She Loves Me*:

"It's a superb story superbly told, an acknowledged glory of the day…….. *She Loves Me* is a classic, because it will always surprise a willing public. Remember my matinee ladies? As *She Loves Me* reaches its curtain, Georg and Amalia are leaving the store on Christmas Eve. They're about to part company. But he knows that he's Dear Friend. And we know that he's

Dear Friend. Now *she* has to know. So he quietly sings to her the words of the letter she composed during "Ice Cream."

Now she knows.

And, as Barbara Cook turned to Daniel Massey with a look at once relieved, ecstatic, and terrified, the Eugene O'Neill Theater broke into tremendous applause even before Cook reached Massey's arms for the curtain tableau."

And here is some of what Mordden has to say about *The Music Man*:

"Now a book scene fixes Hill up with an old crony, who warns him about the local music teacher and librarian, smart and a purist in everything. But Hill's got a band to sell, and he smoothes into "Ya Got Trouble," setting the plot proper in motion. Why, that pool table promises nothing less than the arrival of sin in River City! The good people of the town can only protect themselves by herding their youth into a marching band of ...yes! Seventy-six trombones!

Okay, we've had a startling novelty in the salesmen's rap number, a mock-traditional "opening" chorus of "merry" villagers – Sigmund Romberg gone sour - and the action has kicked in painlessly, naturally. One thing's missing – the romance. No: Here comes the music teacher, to prim, self-righteous "walking" music. Hill follows her, masher-style. We're on.

Clearly, one of "The Music Man's unique qualities is a resuscitation of a culture that, after two world wars, television, and Elvis Presley, had utterly disappeared. Knickers, pianola, cistern, corncrib, dime novels, "so's your old man," stereopticon slides, Montgomery Ward, canoodling, - a goodly portion of the show's content had been retired to the American memory bank by the 1950s. Willson is telling a story that is all but faerie today."

Spending a couple of hours watching a talented company perform one of the classic musicals is one of life's greatest pleasures. If you can't get to a theater, listening to an original cast recording is the next best thing. Or reading one of these books and having the plays come to life on the printed page.

Last Voyages

Robert Louis Stevenson was a sickly man, probably owing to a bronchial malady that confounded nineteenth-century doctors. But in spite of his illness he was a cheerful man, well liked by all who new him. And of course he was a skillful and hard-working writer, who had published *Treasure Island*, *Dr. Jekyll and Mr. Hyde*, and *Kidnapped* before his fortieth birthday.

Stevenson, a native of Scotland, thought his homeland's cold, damp climate was partly to blame for his poor health, and he dreamed of finding relief in the islands of the South Pacific. And why not? Royalties from his writing were substantial, and the world was waiting. So, in mid-1888, he set sail from San Francisco on a chartered 93-foot sailboat, complete with hired captain and crew. He first destination: the Marquesas Islands, more than 3000 miles southwest. Remember, this was 1888, when there was no radio, radar, sonar, or GPS. The sailboat, named the Casco, eventually made it, and Stevenson spent some time on the islands before sailing farther southwest, to the Tuamotus and Tahiti. Then, after spending months at a Tahitian village, the party headed north to Hawaii.

If "the party" consisted of a wealthy author, captain, and crew, this would be just another story of the sea. But Stevenson took along his wife Fanny, his mother Maggie, and his stepson. (His wife was married before.) His mother was barely 10 years older than his wife, who was 10 years older than RLS. With such a cast of characters, you can well imagine the chemistry on board the Casco.

Eventually, and after chartering two more ships, Stevenson explored the western Pacific, finally settling in Samoa, where he built a fine house – and died, at age 44. So Stevenson's expedition was in fact a last voyage.

The tale is told in an interesting book called *Treasured Islands*, written a few years ago by Lowell Holmes, a Professor of Anthropology and an accomplished sailor.

Another "last voyage" is a 1960 movie of the same name, starring Robert Stack and Dorothy Malone. What makes this film notable is the fact that the producers, hearing that the famed liner Ile de France was headed for the scrap yard, decided to film the story of a sinking ocean liner aboard a sinking ocean liner. No mock-up, no computer graphics, no model ship in a Hollywood tank. This was the real deal. When the ocean bursts through the liner's dining-room wall, it looks real because it *is* real. (Actually, fireboats were hired to shoot water through the walls.) Stack and Malone are a couple of vacationing passengers, George Sanders is the ship's captain, and Edmond O'Brien is an engine-room chief. The movie is in color, which is only right, and among the shipboard extras you'll see more than a few Asian faces, as the filming location was in the Sea of Japan.

The cast, by the way, really earned their pay on this shoot. O'Brien and Stack in particular had to slosh their way through sea water repeatedly, and the attractive Dorothy Malone was forced to play her role mostly submerged up to her chin. I doubt that these three ever had a more arduous assignment than *The Last Voyage*.

The Ile de France had achieved notoriety before, rescuing passengers of the Andrea Doria when she sank off Nantucket in 1956. But her movie debut was uncredited. The French Line understandably insisted that all references to the liner's real name be deleted. The ship is called the Claridon in *The Last Voyage*.

An afterthought: In 2012, I took a long cruise to the South Pacific, stopping at many of the islands Stevenson visited over a century before, including the Marquesas, which I found just as entrancing as Stevenson had.

Rules of Civility

The novel is Amor Towles's first, and it's a most impressive debut. Written in the first person, it's a story told, mostly in flashback, by Katie Kontent. As the novel opens, Katie and her husband are touring an exhibition of photographs taken on the New York subway in the 1930s. The subway riders wear faces of urban boredom, which is the point. Katie thinks one of the faces is familiar, then she sees him again in another photograph. Now she is sure: It *is* Tinker Grey. Her husband confirms it, Katie's memory takes over, and the novel is launched.

This is a New York novel, with more than a hint of Scott Fitzgerald's Manhattan in the late 30s. The characters are well insulated from the Depression, privileged people with pieds-a-terre in Manhattan and big homes on Long Island. Katie is a working girl, on the outer fringes of society, but she and her friend Eve parlay good looks and sharp wit to worm their way into the inner circle.

Tinker Grey is at the center of this circle, along with various friends that inhabit the social stratosphere.

The author is a stylist, and a good one. A graduate of Yale and Stanford, he is a principal of a New York investment firm. For a male writer to channel a female memoirist is no small trick, but Towles pulls it off.

Katie is the kind of a girl that today's television would build a sitcom around. She has pithy one-liners galore, and she attracts not only men but women, who collide with her a little too often, given the population of 1938 Manhattan. ("Katie? Katie Kontent? Is that you?") The film rights have been purchased, and we can expect to savor Katie Kontent's trenchant humor one more time.

The title refers to a list of 110 rules of civilized behavior, as drafted by a young George Washington, and printed in an appendix. (No. 65: Speak not injurious Words neither in Jest nor Earnest. Scoff at none although they give Occasion.)

The Painted Veil

S omerset Maugham was a good story-teller, not, in my opinion, a great writer, but a very good story-teller. There's a difference, as I have pointed out in my essays on Waugh and Greene.

Recently a friend recommended a movie based on a Maugham story, *The Painted Veil*. I wasn't able to see the movie (but will one day), but found the story in my library, in a volume called *The Maugham Reader*. At 200 pages, it is longer than the usual Maugham short story, but it is worth the time. Like most of Maugham's work, it is stiffly written, but what a story! It was first made into a movie in 1934, starring Greta Garbo, but the version my friend recommended was the 2006 film, with Naomi Watts, Edward Norton, and Liev Schreiber. The drama takes place in China, and the movie was filmed on location. I thought while reading it that it would have made an excellent subject for Merchant and Ivory.

The story involves a flighty, attractive young English woman who, anxious to be married before her younger sister trots down the aisle, marries a bacteriologist whom she can barely tolerate. The two travel to Hong Kong, where the bacteriologist has a mid-level civil post. Bored, the bride (Kitty) enters into a torrid affair with a British magistrate. The husband, a dull sort (but very intelligent), finds out, and in a confrontational scene agrees to a divorce on two conditions: The lover's wife must also agree (in writing) to a divorce, and the lover must agree to marry Kitty once the decree is final. The bacteriologist is far ahead of his wife in this game: As he expected, the lover wanted Kitty only as a plaything, not a wife, and he is much too ambitious to permit a scandal.

Walter then announces that his research will take him to the interior of China, where there is a cholera epidemic, and he wishes his wife to accompany him. The setup is too good for me to say more.

After reading the fine story, I saw the movie, and it was a disappointment. It is one thing to read about a cholera epidemic on the printed page; it is quite another to see it in all its horrific reality.

Cloudstreet

But here is a book and a television miniseries that are both superb. One should see the miniseries first, then read the book, for reasons that I will get to. But both are extraordinary.

The novel and the six-part miniseries are called *Cloudstreet*, and both are from Australia. The book and the screenplay are by an Australian named Tim Winton. The DVD is available, but it has yet to be seen on American TV. It probably will not satisfy all tastes, but it certainly satisfied mine.

The story involves two families in Western Australia in the 40s and 50s. They are the Lambs and the Pickles, both hit by the depression and by tragedy. Sam Pickles has lost the fingers of one hand in an accident, and the Lambs' youngest son has nearly drowned and is as a result retarded. Sam Pickles inherits a large, ramshackle house near Perth and looks for a family of tenants to share in the upkeep. Enter the Lambs. The spine of the story is the relationship of the two families as the years pass. But it is most assuredly not a soap opera. "It is a story about life," says the book's author, simply.

The book is slow-going for an American reader, and the writing is peppered with Aussie idioms. It is a powerful story, almost poetic in the telling, but, engrossing as the story is, it is the artistry of the director (Matthew Saville) that produces the magic that we see unfold in the DVD. That plus the acting, which is absolutely flawless, and it is all the more striking to an American viewer because the Australian cast is unfamiliar. There is not a weak link in the bunch.

Thus my advice to see the miniseries first. It will not spoil the book, as there is nothing to be spoiled. It is first-class entertainment, from beginning to end.

How can Australia, which has fewer people than Texas, produce such a beautifully crafted television drama? Years ago, the country gave us *A Town Like Alice*, an excellent series based on a Nevil Shute novel, but that was 1981. Maybe there were other great dramas from

Down Under, and I just haven't been paying attention, but I doubt it. But I certainly will be watching from now on, and I have marked Matthew Saville as a name to be reckoned with.

You are unlikely to see Cloudstreet on Masterpiece Theater. The series has several sexually explicit scenes and some four-letter words, and the Aussies would probably not tolerate heavy-handed editing. Too bad; such quality television deserves a large audience.

Joan Leslie

My first love was Joan Leslie. Seeing her on the screen today in one of her old movies, I can easily see why I was so smitten. In the early 1940s she was always typed as the wholesome girl next door, and I wondered why none of the girls who lived next door to me ever looked like Joan Leslie. Then, as she grew a bit older, she was exactly the kind of loyal wife the girl next door could be expected to become. She was the dependable, staunchly supportive better half to George M. Cohan (*Yankee Doodle Dandy*), Sergeant York's girl back home, and a near-miss romance for George Gershwin (*Rhapsody in Blue*).

But her shining hour came when she danced to the Arlen-Mercer ballad "My Shining Hour" with Fred Astaire, in *The Sky's the Limit*. Joan was 17 during the filming, Astaire 44 and a living legend. How did she do?

Just fine. Dance critic John Mueller, in his excellent *Astaire Dancing*, writes that of Astaire's partners in the post Rogers era, "Joan Leslie is most closely reminiscent of Rogers, particularly as an actress: attractive, intelligent, feisty, vulnerable." No one can seriously say that she was as good a dancer as Rogers, but she was better than her 17 years gave anyone the right to expect.

The Sky's the Limit tells the improbable story of a Flying Tigers pilot on leave and trying to score points with a young magazine photo-journalist, who regards him as just another wolf, which he is. (He is dressed in civvies.) Joan's character is named Joan, and Fred's is named Fred, and the chemistry between them works, despite the obvious age difference. After the usual plot complications are resolved, the two are obviously fated to be mated, though first Fred has to fly back across the Pacific to win the war. You could always count on a happy if not downright inspiring ending in 1943. It's a pleasant enough movie, because the two leads are so likeable. A bonus is the appearance of Robert Benchley, one of the era's best humorists, as Joan's boss and Astaire's rival.

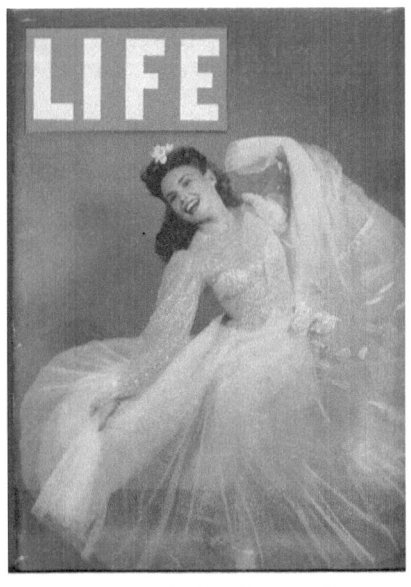

The Sky's the Limit received mixed reviews, but Mueller calls it "one of the most effective and affecting war films Hollywood ever turned out," thanks to its stars, its music, and good script. My only complaint is that there are too few songs. When you have Harold Arlen and Johnny Mercer on the payroll, it makes no sense to settle for just a few musical numbers.

Joan Leslie was not a great actress, or even an especially good one. She was no singer, so her vocals had to be dubbed. As noted, she was a good dancer, and I wish she had more chances to display her footwork. What Joan Leslie had was a sparkling personality, a slightly mischievous smile, a good figure, and a wonderful face, which managed to convey wit and intelligence and style, all rolled together. She was the girl any parents would want their son to marry.

She was also a poster child for the 1940s and the age of innocence. All in all, she appeared in more than 40 movies, most of them fair at best, first as Joan Brodel (the name she was born with), then as Joan Leslie (better). For a while, she was, for the studios, money in the bank, even playing herself in *Hollywood Canteen*. At 17, she was featured on a *Life* cover, a sure sign of stardom.

After the war, as innocence went out of style, so did Joan Leslie. Today, I doubt that one out of 10 people would recognize her name. I try to think of a contemporary actress who is a latter-day version of Joan Leslie, someone I can compare her to, but it is no use; the girl next door doesn't live there any more.

In 1950, Joan Leslie married a doctor, who died in 2000. She has twin daughters, both doctors. Joan is now in her eighties. To me, though, she will always be 17, on the big screen at the Coddy, smiling at me. Just me.

The Scene's the Thing

Every great movie includes some scenes that transcend the movie itself, almost like miniature movies that you can't forget even when, years later, the movie itself slips out of your memory. Even in a so-so movie, one scene can be a treasure. Here are a few scenes I consider among the very best.

Dear Heart (Glen Ford, Geraldine Page)

Ford is a businessman who has been transferred to New York and is staying at a Manhattan hotel while looking for an apartment. The same hotel is host to a postmasters' convention, and spinster postmistress Page and Ford meet when they are asked to share a table at lunch. After a friendship develops, Ford asks for Page's help in checking out apartments, with her feminine eye presumably standing in for that of his fiancée. Page is convinced it is all a ruse and that Ford is preparing to declare himself for her. As they inspect the apartment, Page slowly realizes that Ford really does have a fiancée en route from Ohio. Only an actress of Page's skill could make this soap-opera moment a scene of high tragedy. (That Henry Mancini theme doesn't hurt a bit, either.)

All About Eve (Bette Davis, Gary Merrill)

The ultimate backstage drama, with dialog that snaps, crackles, and pops all along the way. My favorite scene has Margo Channing (Bette Davis) arriving late for rehearsal and finding that director Gary Merrill has run the scene with Margo's new understudy, Eve (Anne Baxter). The thought that Margo should need an understudy, especially when the understudy is the devious Eve, is too much. Davis delivers a barrage of poisonous barbs at Merrill, the writer, the producer, and everyone else in range. Exasperated playwright Lloyd Richards (Hugh Marlowe) wonders, "When will the piano realize that it hasn't written the concerto?"

The Final Cut

The Caine Mutiny (Humphrey Bogart, Jose Ferrer)

This film is filled with great scenes, but the best is saved
for last, when Captain Queeg (Humphrey Bogart) is
called to testify at the mutiny trial of Lieutenant Maryk
(Van Johnson). Defense attorney Jose Ferrer must walk a
tight-rope: His client's case requires that he expose
Queeg as psychotic, but the military tribunal will not
permit a frontal attack on a fellow officer. So the
attorney patiently baits his trap, and Queeg self-
destructs. Compelling drama.

The Hustler (Jackie Gleason, Paul Newman)

The high-stakes pool game between "Fast Eddie" Felson
(Paul Newman) and Minnesota Fats (Jackie Gleason) is
a classic, with an oh-so-wise Gleason watching the
cocky, oh-so-talented Newman, waiting for Felson to
fold under pressure. This is one of those films that had to
be filmed in black and white; a Technicolor poolroom
would have been terribly wrong. Newman and Piper
Laurie are great, but it is Gleason, who doesn't have that
many lines, who steals every scene he's in.

Soldier in the Rain (Jackie Gleason, Tuesday Weld)

Gleason again, this time as Master Sergeant Maxwell
Slaughter, a career soldier who is befriended by a
younger noncom, Eustace Clay (Steve McQueen).
Eustace, sure that his top kick needs female
companionship, arranges a date with Bobby Jo

44

Pepperdine (Tuesday Weld). They go to a carnival. Slaughter, whose taste runs to crossword puzzles, has nothing in common with the bobby-soxer, and he is obviously bored stiff. Then, little by little, he realizes that Bobby Jo is a good, if scatter-brained, person, and boredom turns into the milk of human kindness, if just for the moment. Slaughter is not looking for romance, and in the film he doesn't find it, but that carnival scene is a treat.

Separate Tables (Deborah Kerr, David Niven)

Terence Rattigan just cannot write a bad play, it seems, and this is a corker. It all takes place in a British seaside resort, out of season. The long-term guests include David Niven, a retired Army Major with an endless supply of war stories and Deborah Kerr, as Sybil, the mousy daughter of a domineering mother, played by the wonderful Gladys Cooper. Niven is found to have committed an indiscretion at a local theater, and Dame Gladys spearheads a movement to oust the Major from the hotel. As the votes are cast, Deborah finds her courage and her voice, siding with the major in the pivotal dining-room scene. Another incredible outing by Kerr, and Niven's well deserved Oscar.

The Americanization of Emily (James Garner, Julie Andrews, Joyce Grenfell)

This superb, underrated movie stars James Garner as an Admiral's aide and Julie Andrews as Emily, a volunteer driver in WW2 London. The two are dynamite together, and the film is essentially a love story with an anti-war message as counterpoint. This message is delivered with great wit and style, with Garner wryly suggesting that the more statues we build to honor war heroes, the more wars we will fight to produce more heroes and more statues. The scene I like best belongs to Joyce Grenfell (Emily's mother), who spars with Garner over the morality of war, with daughter Emily a fascinated onlooker. Grenfell plays the dotty lady to a tee, and Garner oozes irony. The razor-sharp script was written by Paddy Chayefsky.

Fanny (Maurice Chevalier, Charles Boyer)

I like this movie for many reasons, including the glorious color photography of Marseilles and the always delectable Leslie Caron, but the highlight for me is the verbal jousting between Cesar (Charles Boyer) and Panisse (Maurice Chevalier). Cesar is the father of Marius, who has run off to sea, leaving Fanny pregnant. Panisse, an aged, wealthy sail maker, offers to marry Fanny and give the baby a proper father, and he is accepted. Cesar and Panisse, two old codgers played by two marvelous actors, go jaw to jaw over the propriety of the marriage, and their scenes together are just wonderful. Director Joshua Logan wisely decided to let the strong story have center stage, using Harold Rome's score (for the Broadway musical) simply as background music.

The Final Cut

The Band Wagon (Fred Astaire, Jack Buchanan)

My favorite movie musical is *The Band Wagon*, in which Fred Astaire, as an over-the-hill star of movie musicals, is lured to New York to star in a play written by Oscar Levant and Nanette Fabray (Comden and Green writing characters based on themselves). Cyd Charisse is the co-star, and Jack Buchanan is the "important" director who aims to turn a musical trifle into a serious Faustian drama. The dress rehearsal, in which everything goes horribly awry, is very funny. And the Astaire-Charisse dance to "Dancing in the Dark" is exquisite.

Avalon (Armin Mueller-Stahl. Lou Jacobi)

Thanksgiving dinner marks the major annual gathering of the Jewish family at the core of this fine movie, and when the family moves to a new neighborhood in Baltimore, uncle Gabe, a long-time regular, arrives late. So the patriarch, Sam, decides to start without him and carves the turkey. Gabe (Lou Jacobi) then enters, and he can't believe his eyes. "You cut the turkey without me?" he erupts. A major family breakup is thus threatened – because "you cut the turkey without me." There are many other great scenes in this must-see film, but the Thanksgiving dinner brings it all home.

Lolita (James Mason, Shelley Winters)

Shelley Winters (who, referring to her cameo in *The Poseidon Adventure*, said "It ain't over till the fat lady swims") was never better than in *Lolita*, in which she played the nymphet's mother, Charlotte Haze. Charlotte, acting the sophisticate, is first seen trying to convince Professor Humbert (James Mason) to rent a spare room in her house. She tries to impress him with idiotic references to artists, dropping names like "Van Gock" along the way. It gets better when Humbert rents the room and Charlotte sets her cap for him.

The Third Man (Joseph Cotten, Valli)

The Third Man is an out-and-out masterpiece. It has one riveting scene after another, but the one that I remember most vividly takes place at night, on a Vienna street. Holly Martins (Joseph Cotten) has been investigating the apparent death of old friend Harry Lime at that very spot, and he had questioned the apartment porter, a witness to the traffic accident. Now the porter has been murdered, and his small son, remembering Martins's earlier visit, points him out, crying "Murderer." The little boy's big, round face is one you'll never forget. You also will never forget the ending, Valli's long walk at the cemetery, with the zither strumming in the background.

Shane (Alan Ladd, Jack Palance)

The climax of *Shane* is, of course, the gunfight between Shane (Alan Ladd) and Jack Wilson (Jack Palance). But before that, there is a scene that defines Wilson as not only fast on the draw, but evil. A headstrong homesteader, Frank Torrey (Elisha Cook, Jr.) squares off against Wilson, although he is clearly outmatched. Wilson, knowing that Torrey calls himself "Stonewall," insults his southern heritage, while the skies darken. Wilson is on a platform, looking down on the hapless Torrey, standing in the mud puddles. Without this setup, the Shane-Wilson climax would have been less powerful. But it is the over-all look of the scene – the sky, the tiny town in the middle of nowhere, the muddy streets, the scruffy dog, all contributing to the sense of impending doom, that makes this a great film moment.

No claim is made that these are the greatest scenes in all moviedom. Hundreds more could be listed, from *Casablanca, Gone With the Wind, Doctor Zhivago, Sunset Boulevard, A Star is Born*, and so many other movies. The next time you are watching a good movie and are captivated by a particular scene, mentally bookmark it.

The Producers

The Red Sox game ends early, so there is time for a movie before turning in. I pull out the latest DVD from Netflix, a movie called *The Matador*, with Pierce Brosnan and Greg Kinnear. The sleeve says it is only 1 hour and 30 minutes long. Perfect.

I use the menu to bypass the commercials and hit "play movie." The screen fills with the announcement that the source of this entertainment is:

The Weinstein Company

A water scene appears, then a city skyline, to suggest, no doubt, that this movie does not come from any fly-by-night studio, but from one of the financial centers of America.

MIRAMAX FILMS

the screen then says. Fade to black. Then:

STRATUS FILM COMPANY

I remember Stratus as a computer company, which was bought by some other computer company. Must be a different Stratus. When do we get to the movie? Then:

DEJ PRODUCTIONS

I look at my watch. Is all this included in the advertised 90 minutes? Then:

EQUITY PARTNERS

the screen reports, in big letters. Again, fade to black, then:

STRATUS FILM COMPANY & DEJ PRODUCTIONS PRESENT

What does this combination present? Why, another title, of course. This time:

IN ASSOCIATION WITH EQUITY PARTNERS

MEDIAFONDS GmbH & Co. KG II

German money at work, I figure. Still no sign of the movie. The litany goes on:

A FURST FILMS IRISH DREAMTIMES PRODUCTION

The Germans and the Irish have teamed up, it seems, with a bunch of Hollywood venture capitalists. One imagines that their lawyers argued for hours over the order of these credits, and the size of type. Then:

A FILM BY RICHARD SHEPARD

Then, finally, the opening scene.

Somehow, I manage to watch the whole movie, hoping that it will justify the preliminaries. It does not. In fact, the movie is plain dreadful, leading me to postulate Van Veen's first law of cinema: The quality of the movie is inversely proportional to the length of the opening credits.

Two by Streep

Going to the movies can be a painful experience. If you arrive 10 minutes early, you have to endure 10 minutes of inane commercials and trivia quizzes asking you questions about "personalities" you never heard of. There are slides exhorting you not to talk during the movie (generally ignored), not to litter the theater with trash (also ignored), and to turn off cell phones (ditto). Then a few trailers, then, finally, the feature film.

This week we endured all this not once, but twice, at two different theaters. This was a cosmic event, not unlike an eclipse of Pluto by Venus. I doubt that we have been this venturesome in at least 20 years. The results were mixed.

Both films featured performances by Meryl Streep, and she was the main attraction that drew us to the theaters. I thought I'd enjoy one of the movies, endure the other.

The Final Cut

This was the way it worked out, though not in the order I expected.

The first was *The Devil Wears Prada*. It was a good movie, and Jill and I thoroughly enjoyed it. In *Prada*, Streep plays Miranda Priestly, the all-powerful editor of the fashion magazine *Runway*. Anne Hathaway, just out of Northwestern with a journalism degree, applies for the job of Miranda's second assistant, a job, she is repeatedly told, that most girls would kill for. Her character, Andrea, dresses for comfort, not style, which invites the scorn of everyone at *Runway*, most notably the first assistant, Emily (well played by Emily Blunt).

Somehow, Andrea lands the job, and she eventually decides to take her position, Miranda, and *Runway* seriously and join the fashion parade. Success at *Runway* distances her from her Joe-Sixpack boyfriend. At a major fashion event in Paris, Andrea is forced to reflect on life's choices. Will she succumb to the world of *haut couture* and seize the huge opportunity Miranda offers her, or will she chuck it all to reclaim Joe Sixpack and his *bas couture* persona? If you don't know the answer to this question you are culturally challenged.

Other assets: the script, filled with zingers; Stanley Tucci, playing a top creative talent at *Runway*; and Florian Ballhaus's stunning cinematography. The nighttime shots of Manhattan and Paris are just breathtaking.

The debits: the story stretches plausibility to the limit; the plot is predictable every step of the way; and the music is strictly for the MTV crowd. But it is a solid movie, worth seeing - and much better than I expected. The most telling tribute is this: In a theater filled with mostly women, some carrying cell phones and many with large tubs of popcorn, there was not a sound to be heard during the screening of the film.

Now, to the other movie: *Prairie Home Companion,* a Robert Altman film that takes place entirely in the Fitzgerald Theater in St. Paul Minnesota, during what we are told is the final performance of Garrison Keillor's popular radio show. (A venal Texas businessman is planning to raze the theater in favor of a parking lot.)

I am a big fan of Keillor and PHC, and I entered the theater in Portland expecting to be enchanted. I wasn't. In fact, I marvel at Mr. Altman's ability to take a cracking good radio show, with characters like Guy Noir, Keillor's wonderfully nostalgic monologues, virtuoso turns by talented musicians, and the commercials for duct tape, ketchup, and powder milk biscuits, and turn it all into a boring movie. The music was not as good as we hear every Saturday, the monologues were missing, the humor was flat. Meryl Streep and Lily Tomlin, as a country music sister act (Yolanda and Rhonda Johnson), were fine, but Kevin Kline's Guy Noir was dull as dirt, and Tommy Lee Jones, with about 11 lines, was wasted. The editing was especially annoying, jumping from stage to backstage and interrupting the flow of most of the songs. The cinematography was depressingly dark, as if the theater's projector needed a new bulb. The story line was equally dark, with Yolanda's teen-aged daughter writing poems about suicide and the angel of death carrying off one of the old-timers on the show. Regular listeners to PHC know that Keillor's world is grounded in Norwegian sobriety, cold, dark Minnesota winters, and Lutheran morality, but his stories always turnout to be essentially warm and witty. The movie, alas, was neither.

In sum, *Prairie Home Companion* is a loser, despite the incandescent Meryl. Not even she can overcome material this bad. Listen to the radio show; it's far, far better.

The Disney Touch

I watch movies, not to be educated or manipulated or shocked, but to be entertained. Measured by that standard, Disney's *Enchanted* was a success. The story line, if you don't know it already, goes like this: Giselle, a fair maiden living in a cartoonland called Andalasia, is in love with a handsome prince named Edward. Edward's stepmother, the queen, fears that Giselle will be a rival for her throne, so she throws her down a wishing well to a place where there are no happy-ever-afters – New York City.

Giselle, now played by the flesh-and-blood Amy Adams, clambers out of a manhole in Times Square and is immediately surrounded by the horrors of Gotham. She is rescued from danger by a passerby named Robert. He is a lawyer and a single dad, living with his little daughter Morgan, and the trio repair to Robert's apartment until he figures out what to do with this confused young woman dressed like a princess in a fairy tale. Eventually, Prince Edward also makes the trip from cartoonland to New York in search of his true love, who is learning the way people in the real world go about courting. The queen, keeping an evil eye on things from Andalasia, isn't crazy about these developments and dispatches a minion to dispatch Giselle.

You get the idea: Animated characters are thrust into the real world, learn some lessons and teach some, too. In this case, Giselle from Andalasia and Robert from New York City fall in love and are obviously fated to live happily ever after.

Woody Allen also arranged for a handsome movie actor to step out of a movie to fall in love with a downtrodden housewife in the audience. The movie was *The Purple Rose of Cairo*, and it was clever and enjoyable. It was set in the Great Depression, and it exploited the contrast between the on-screen characters in a drawing-room comedy and the dreary moviegoers seeking escape from hard times. In *Enchanted*, no one is conspicuously miserable. Robert is a successful lawyer living in a luxurious Manhattan apartment. But his life is empty. Morgan, his little girl, wants a fairy-tale pop-up book, but her father gives her a coffee-table book on famous women like Rosa Parks and Madam Curie. He doesn't do fairy tales.

Enchanted, given that plot, could have been sappy. Instead it is, well, enchanting. It has something Woody Allen, with all his talent, could never have.

That something is the Disney touch.

Talk about a brand for the ages! The screen fills with the glorious colors of the magic kingdom, against the strains of "When You Wish Upon a Star." Then the narrator, Julie Andrews, sets up the story with the aid of a pop-up book of fairy tales, a device that will be revisited at the end of the movie. It had to be Julie Andrews. The adorable Amy Adams looks very much like Julie playing Cinderella in the Rodgers and Hammerstein TV special so many years ago, and of course Julie has That Voice.

The Disney touch also fills the screen with the usual menagerie of happy-go-lucky computer-generated animals, including a chipmunk who does his best to protect Giselle from harm. The movie is also chock-full of references to earlier Disney classics. The queen is a dead take-off of the queen in *Snow White*, as is her *alter ego*, the old hag who offers Snow White (and now Giselle) a poison apple. On one level, this latest Disney hit is making fun of all the Disney golden oldies. Only a film studio with monumental self-confidence would dare to do that.

Most of the movie takes place in New York, with real people, and the Disney touch is just as magical here. A long musical scene in Central Park involves dozens if not hundreds of dancers (there are certainly more than 100 dancers named in the end credits), and the obligatory ball scene at the climax is Disney at its best.

A word must be said in praise of the two actors who play Giselle's suitors. As world-weary lawyer Robert, Patrick Dempsey has a tough assignment. When he is on screen, Giselle is usually with him, which means no one (no man, certainly) is looking at him. His dialogue is mostly straight lines, though every now and then the writers give him a gem. He is absolutely perfect in the role. James Marsden, who plays Prince Edward, is given a showy costume and a sword to brandish, and he must have had great fun hamming it up. The make-up crew and the costumers should also be credited for making the cartoon characters and their worldly counterparts look reasonably alike. (They obviously had no trouble sounding alike.)

I don't want to give the impression that *Enchanted* is flawless. First, while I accept that birds and chipmunks and even caterpillars can sing and dance in the magic kingdom, I can't buy lovable rats and cockroaches. (No, I didn't like Pixar's *Ratatouille*.) Second, the over-the-top finale, with the queen transforming herself into a huge dragon and then climbing a skyscraper, King Kong style, struck me as pointless. In *Snow White*, the queen/hag with her poison apple were quite enough. Maybe the Disney folks thought a modern audience needed a heavier dose of shock and awe, but I thought the last 10 minutes of the movie (after the exquisite ball scene) was a misfire.

Still, the pluses outweighed the minuses, and the movie was a winner.

Once upon a time, long long ago, I saw the original *Snow White*, and in the years since I have seen most of the animated Disney classics and have visited Disneyland with my children. There is nothing like the Disney experience, because it taps into a very deep, very primal feeling that there must be someplace where dreams really do come true. I'll let the psychologists and the theologians sort that out, but what I know is that for me, the Disney magic hasn't worn off, after so many years. It just keeps on living happily ever after.

The Lubitsch Touch

The Wall Street Journal headlined an article on this year's crop of Oscar nominees "Fade to Bleak," the point being that four of the five movies were grim stories, filled with blood and gore, amplified by modern technology that lets you actually see grizzly scenes of throat-slashing and other explicitly portrayed mayhem. One of the contenders is aptly named *There Will Be Blood*, so you can't say you weren't warned. So much for the movie theater as a place to escape the hard realities of life.

Once upon a time, it was different. In the early thirties, the public's appetite for escape via movie musicals was insatiable. Some of them were awful, but some were excellent, thanks to performers like Maurice Chevalier, Jeanette MacDonald, and, from England, Jack Buchanan. On the stage, *The Desert Song*, *The Student Prince*, *The New Moon*, etc. were still hugely popular, so it is not surprising that the plots for many of these musicals were essentially Hollywood's versions of European operettas. By today's standards, they are silly stories, but then, they are no sillier than most of what's now playing at the local Cineplex. The other night I watched, for as long as I could stand it, a recent flick called *Mr. Brooks*, starring Kevin Costner and William Hurt. The plot was at least as noncredible as the worst of the operettas, and there was no music to offset the stupidity.

The master of the romantic-comedy genre in the early 30s was Ernst Lubitsch, and the term "the Lubitsch touch" is still applied to the most stylish romantic comedies.

Some of the Lubitsch treasures have recently been released on DVD. I recently waded in, and I'm glad I did. Here is what I found.

The Love Parade

The first 10 minutes of this film telegraph the whimsy that is to follow. Maurice Chevalier (whose name appears above the title) is a diplomat attached to the Sylvanian embassy in Paris. (He has been there long enough to have acquired his French accent, along with a string of female companions.) As we enter the scene, we hear an argument behind closed doors. His girlfriend has found a garter, and it isn't hers. As she and Chevalier argue about the garter, her husband enters and sizes up the situation. Disgraced, she finds a revolver, shoots herself, and falls to the floor. The grief-stricken husband takes the gun from her hand and shoots Chevalier. But Chevalier, reprising a much-practiced scene, has loaded the gun with blanks. The husband, overjoyed to find his wife unharmed, exits with her (but not before she asks Chevalier to zip up her dress).

The Sylvanian ambassador, fed up with Chevalier's string of scandals, sends him back to Sylvania, ruled by a beautiful but lonely Queen Louise, played by Jeanette MacDonald in her first movie role. The rest of the story is thoroughly predictable. Comic relief, such as it is, is provided by British vaudevillian Lupino Lane (Ida Lupino's uncle) and, in her cutesy period, Lillian Roth. The score, by Victor Schertzinger, features one standard, "Dream Lover." The production is amazing for 1929, and the audio and video on the DVD are not bad, considering.

My mother was a big fan of Maurice Chevalier, and it is easy to see why. His warm personality and pleasant singing voice must have been dynamite to the audiences of 1929. As a matter of fact, they were all still evident three decades later, in *Gigi*.

Monte Carlo

The girl is still Jeanette MacDonald, but the male lead is now British song and dance man Jack Buchanan. Jeanette is a countess who runs out on her wedding to an old, dim-witted nobleman and flees to Monte Carlo, where she falls under the spell of a hairdresser named Rudolph. But we know that Rudolph is really a count who pretends to be a hairdresser in order to meet the beautiful Jeanette. She is nearly broke (though she is attended by a maid and a retinue of other servants), and a big win at the casino is her only hope.

The plot unfolds as in *The Love Parade*. She spurns him, he spurns her, she comes to her senses, etc. The similarity with the other movie is easily explained: Lubitsch, once he found a winning formula, milked it. In *The Love Parade*, the climactic scene is a ballet at the royal theater, with Queen Louise and her Prince Consort in the seats of honor. In *Monte Carlo*, the climactic scene is an opera (a contrived "Monseur Beaucaire") with the Countess and Rudolph attending. The score for the film (including the opera scene) was written by Richard Whiting, and it contains one standard: "Beyond the Blue Horizon." My wife reminds me that when this song was played during WW2, the final words, "a rising sun" were replaced by "a setting sun" in a burst of Nipponophobia.

One other song is worth mention: "Always in All Ways." It is a delightfully catchy tune, well performed by Buchanan and MacDonald. And Buchanan, like Chevalier, kept rolling along, delivering a knockout performance 23 years later in one of the best musicals ever screened, *The Band Wagon*.

One Hour With You

If you want to find out why Maurice Chevalier was the hottest property at Paramount in the early thirties, catch this one. It is a delicious Lubitsch confection, with clever dialogue, a few good songs, and Chevalier at his comedic best, which is saying a lot.

The opening is memorable: The chief of the Paris police orders his gendarmes to sweep the City's parks of its lovers, not because he is against necking, but because the economy suffers when people are on park benches instead of spending money in nightclubs. Chevalier and MacDonald are among the park bench smoochers, and they are expelled by a dutiful officer. But they are married, and they are madly in love with each other, as Chevalier tells us in one of his arch to-the-camera asides. What a setup for the bedroom farce that is to follow, when Jeanette's best friend, the sexy Mitzi, comes to visit! The supporting cast includes Roland Young as Mitzi's cuckolded husband and Charlie Ruggles as an old friend who has a yen for Jeanette. The writers have given them some very funny lines, and they both deliver the goods.

The music includes two songs you will recognize, if you're old enough: the title tune and "Day After Day" (we will always be sweethearts). The music is fine, and the cast (including the lovely Genevieve Tobin as Mitzi, the blonde hypotenuse of the triangle) is first-rate. But to me the revelation was Chevalier. I knew he could put over a song, but I never knew he had such a natural talent for comedy.

The Smiling Lieutenant

Another operetta-based musical starring Maurice Chevalier. This one, made in 1931, before the censors were at work, has a plot that is silly even by operetta standards, but it's a lot of fun all the same. Niki (Chevalier), a lieutenant in the Austrian army, is in love with Franzi (Claudette Colbert), a violinist and the leader of a girls' band. While on duty as an honor guard to greet the visiting king and princess of neighboring Flausenthurm, he smiles at Franzi but is thought to be making eyes at Princess Anna (Miriam Hopkins) and is soon forced to marry her. Thus the triangle: the smiling Niki, Franzi the violinist, and Anna of Flausenthurm. Complications follow, and Lubitsch keeps you guessing till the end whether Niki will wind up with the blonde Anna or the brunette Franzi. The only musical number worth mentioning is "Jazz Up Your Lingerie," notable mostly for the pianos backing up Hopkins and Colbert.

The dialogue is good. The king begins his grilling of the lieutenant by demanding that he spell Flausenthurm (he has been irritated by a missing "h" in an Austrian sign), and when Chevalier spells it correctly, the ladies in waiting swoon. ("That boy knows his alphabet.") As I said, it's all too silly for words, but once you accept that, it's not bad. To audiences in the depth of the Great Depression, it must have been a wonderful tonic.

Trouble in Paradise

Trouble in Paradise is a Lubitsch romantic comedy, sans music, and it is revered by movie buffs for its sophistication and pre-Code sexiness. Debonair Herbert Marshall and Miriam Hopkins are jewel thieves, and Kay Francis is the wealthy mark. It's all played for laughs – not belly laughs, but laughs from naughty situations, double entendres, etc. It is like an extended

Cole Porter lyric turned into a movie. Today's directors should study it, in order to learn that a movie can be very racy without showing naked couples rolling about in the hay. In fact, without the dialogue this could be a G-rated movie. It could also have been a musical, and in fact I wish it were. I don't know whether Marshall and company could sing, but I think the Lubitsch touch is deftest when set to music.

These movies probably will not appeal to younger audiences. They are by definition "dated," they are of course in black and white, and the appeal lies in the dialogue, the situations, and, sometimes, the music. Almost all scenes are interiors, typically within palaces. There are no car chases, airplane crashes, or murders. But for anyone, young or old, who is interested in movies as an art form, Lubitsch 101 is a must course.

Gems by Pollack and Wilder

Sydney Pollack directed some mediocre movies, some fair movies, and a couple that are flat-out gems. One deserves to be on anyone's "ten best" list. It is *Out of Africa*, and it is so good that, despite its length, it wears well with a second or third viewing. How Pollack put it all together staggers the imagination, but one factoid illustrates his determination to get it right: Though the film was shot in Kenya, Pollack wanted animals that were not available locally, so he shipped them in by air from Europe!

Meryl Streep as Karen Blixen owns the picture, but the supporting cast is brilliant, especially Klaus Maria Brandauer as Karen's husband. And Pollack gives us one terrific scene after another, set against the majestic African landscape. The script is solid, and John Barry's score is luscious. The tale is a sad one, ending with Blixen returning to Denmark, leaving behind her dead lover (Robert Redford) and her beloved native servants. But some sad (a better word would be "poignant") stories leave you somehow uplifted, moved by the knowledge that you've just watched larger-than-life characters doing important things. Directing this movie must have been a Herculean undertaking, and off this one project Pollack ranks among the very best.

Most critics have given *Out of Africa* its due, and it deservedly won a Best Picture Oscar, but another Pollack film came and went without much notice, which is too bad because it, too, is Pollack at the top of his game. This was the 1995 remake of *Sabrina*.

Usually, I don't see the point of remakes unless the original was a bad telling of a good story. But good movies are often recycled even though the original was just fine. I liked Judy Garland and James Mason in *A Star Is Born*, but I liked their predecessors, Janet Gaynor and Frederic March, at least as much. I thought *Showboat* with Irene Dunne was better than the later film with Kathryn Grayson and everyone on the MGM lot. Marlon Brando, good as he is, couldn't match Clark

Gable in *Mutiny on the Bounty*, nor could the talented Steve Martin compare with Spencer Tracy in *Father of the Bride*. The list goes on, but you get the idea.

But the original *Sabrina* was a badly flawed reworking of a witty Samuel Taylor play (*Sabrina Fair*), and it deserved another chance. All right, the original had Audrey Hepburn, but that is all it had. Humphrey Bogart and William Holden, two excellent actors, were horribly miscast as a tycoon and his playboy kid brother – just how miscast you realize when you see Pollack's 1995 version. Here Harrison Ford is believable as a captain of industry, and Greg Kinnear, a TV actor making his film debut, is more than believable; he's perfect.

Julia Ormond is no Audrey Hepburn, but she is a fine Sabrina – pretty and vulnerable, as she should be, in this Cinderella story of the chauffeur's daughter and the millionaire. The color cinematography is a feast for the eyes (Paris, Long Island, Martha's Vinyard). Best of all, Pollack resisted the temptation to "sex it up" for the juveniles in the audience. You can poke a few holes in the plot, but so what? This is a romantic comedy, where you don't analyze; you sit back and enjoy.

Another Samuel Taylor play that must be mentioned here is *Avanti!*, directed not by Sydney Pollack but by Billy Wilder. In fact, this may be the best of all the Wilder movies, if the least known and the most underrated. The plot: Important Businessman Wendell Armbruster, Jr. (Jack Lemmon) flies to Italy to collect the body of his father and bring it back to Baltimore for a big funeral. The old man, who died on vacation in Ischia, was head of Armbruster Industries, a major corporation, and the funeral will be sized accordingly. En route to Ischia, Lemmon meets Pamela Piggott (Juliet Mills, of the theatrical Mills family), who is headed to Ischia to claim her mother's body. It develops, to Armbruster's (a) disbelief and (b) horror, that the two dead people have been trysting for years in Ischia and died together in a car crash.

That much alone is a pretty good framework for a play, but there's much more. The unctuous hotel manager (played wonderfully by Clive Revill) is one of several characters that will stick with you long after you've seen the movie: a valet who is shot by a housemaid because he done her wrong, a family of farmers who steal the bodies for ransom, an officious coroner with his ever-ready rubber stamp, the restaurant maitre d' (who, when the dieting Pamela orders an apple for dinner, asks, obsequiously, "Shall I peel it for you?").

In fact, it's a hugely enjoyable movie, with gorgeous scenery and evocative Neapolitan music. Unfortunately, Lemmon is as miscast as a business big wheel as Humphrey Bogart was in *Sabrina*. He is too edgy, sort of like the kind of irritable scold he played in *The Out of Towners*. Wilder should have informed Lemmon that not all successful businessmen are pathological cranks (see Ford, Harrison, in *Sabrina)*. But that minor complaint aside, this is one delicious movie, not to be missed.

Brideshead Regurgitated

In 1947 MGM invited Evelyn Waugh to Hollywood to discuss the sale of the film rights to *Brideshead Revisited*. Soon after talks began, it was clear to Waugh that MGM wanted, not his masterpiece, but a Hollywood version of the story. So the talks broke down. But Waugh made the most of his trip, visiting Forest Lawn Cemetery, which inspired him to write the satirical *The Loved One*. This one was sold to MGM, many years later, with sorry results. Waugh hated it and probably felt relieved that he had at least kept *Brideshead* out of MGM's clutches.

(Actually, Waugh didn't sell the film rights to *The Loved One* to Hollywood. His agent sold them to a Mexican on the assurance that it would never be produced but would allow Waugh and Alec Guinness to enjoy a Mexican holiday together. The Mexican later sold the rights to Hollywood.)

As a matter of fact, Waugh's stylish prose does not translate well to film, the towering exception being the 1981 television production of *Brideshead Revisited*. *Sword of Honor*, based on Waugh's wartime trilogy, was made into a passable TV film, *A Handful of Dust* was okay, and *Scoop* was more than passable, but *Vile Bodies (Bright Young Things)* and *The Loved One* were dreadful. Once the screenwriter decides to "modernize" Waugh, the die is cast: After you remove Waugh's

70

brilliant prose, there is nothing left, because Evelyn Waugh wrote novels, not film treatments. (Graham Greene, on the other hand, wrote with the camera in mind, which is why *The Third Man, The Heart of the Matter, Our Man in Havana*, and other Greene titles were as successful as movies as they were as books.)

Writer John Mortimer, who wrote the screenplay for the widely and justly praised *Brideshead Revisited* miniseries, was rigorously faithful to Waugh's novel, and this fact, plus a solid gold cast, made that production what is, in the minds of many, the best piece of dramatic fiction ever put on film. Laurence Olivier and Claire Bloom were Lord and Lady Marchmain, Jeremy Irons, in his breakthrough role, was Charles Ryder, John Gielgud played his father, and Anthony Andrews was Sebastian Flyte. The supporting actors, notably Simon Jones as Brideshead and Phoebe Nicholls as Cordelia Flyte, were all excellent. But the lion's share of the credit belongs to John Mortimer for capturing not only the language but the spirit of the novel.

That brings me to the 2008 movie version of *Brideshead Revisited*. I was not expecting a production to rival the 1981 TV classic; that would be asking too much. But the lead screenwriter was Andrew Davies, well known and respected for his many Masterpiece Theater scripts, so I was not expecting a total disaster either. But that is what I got. If I had viewed the "Making Of" featurette in the bonus material, I would have been warned. "We wanted to do a contemporary reading of the novel," said someone. Oh-oh. Translation: The producers said to the writers, "Look, Waugh leaves the relationship between Charles and Sebastian ambiguous. Let's make them conspicuously gay, maybe have them kiss. And Waugh's Lady Marchmain is a sympathetic if over-zealous matriarch. Bo-ring. Let's make her a sort of a Catholic dragon lady, with a hint of Lady Macbeth."

The movie is constrained by its length (about two hours), so Anthony Blanche, Cordelia, and Samgrass are reduced to walk-ons. That's forgivable, but not the jettisoning of the spiritual story at the heart of the novel.

For the miniseries, Mortimer was wise enough to have Charles Ryder deliver voice-overs, with the sepulchral voice of Jeremy Irons intoning the elegant sentences of Waugh. Thus, when Ryder, a wartime soldier, returns to the majestic Brideshead mansion he recalls:

"I had been there before; first with Sebastian more than twenty years ago on a cloudless day in June, when the ditches were white with fool's-parsley and meadowsweet and the air heavy with all the scents of summer; it was a day of peculiar splendor, such as our climate affords once or twice a year, when leaf and flower and bird and sun-lit stone and shadow seem all to proclaim the beauty of God; and though I had been there so often, in so many moods, it was to that first visit that my heart returned on this, my latest."

Matthew Goode, who plays Charles in the new film, looks and sounds a bit like Irons, and several other members of the cast look eerily like their earlier counterparts, with similar hairdos and costumes. And Castle Howard in Yorkshire, which became a tourist magnet a quarter century ago after it gained word-wide fame as TV's Brideshead, is again pressed into service for the film. But these surface similarities only remind viewers who have seen the miniseries what a gulf in quality separates the two versions.

The real losers are those whose first exposure to *Brideshead Revisited* is the 2008 film – those who have never read the novel or seen the miniseries. They are to be pitied, for they will wonder, "Why has so much been made of this very ordinary story about very unhappy people?"

In fact, the new film is probably the very film that MGM moguls wanted to make when they welcomed Evelyn Waugh to Hollywood in 1947. They might have cast Cary Grant as Charles, Jimmy Stewart as Sebastian, and Vivien Leigh as Julia. The 1947 movie would have been chaste, of course, but it would have been as soul-less as the newest version. Waugh saw it coming and fled. Too bad his estate didn't have his good taste.

Oh well, at least it hasn't been made into an Andrew Lloyd Webber musical.

The Grass Harp

C ollin Fenwick, orphaned at age 11, is taken in by the Talbo sisters, spinsters, in a southern town in the 1930s. One sister, Verena, owns half the businesses in town. The other, Dolly, is a dreamer and, in the opinion of many, not all there. Dolly likes to roam the fields and collect herbs, roots, and other ingredients for her secret "dropsy cure" medicine. Verena and her fast-talking boyfriend, a "Doctor" Morris Ritz from Chicago, want to commercialize this medicine, but Dolly resists. Dolly's constant companion on her quests for ingredients is a black housekeeper, Catherine. A retired judge, Charlie Cool, has long admired Dolly from afar, for only he (and young Collin) can see that underneath Dolly's simple manner lies a very deep, very wonderful person.

That's the canvas on which Truman Capote painted a novella called *The Grass Harp* over a half century ago. It then became a play, then a musical, and then, in 1996, a movie that was all but ignored at the time. It featured a first-rate cast (Piper Laurie, Sissy Spacek, Walter Matthau, Jack Lemmon, Roddy McDowall, Nell Carter, Mary Steenburgen), a good screenplay by Stirling Silliphant, evocative old-south photography, and hauntingly beautiful background music. The acting is topnotch, the characters well drawn, the best of Capote's flavorful dialog faithfully captured.

But it is Piper Laurie, as Dolly, who dominates this movie, and I think it is an injustice that she was not even nominated for the Best Actress Oscar. She is, in a word, enchanting, and if you think of her as Paul Newman's embittered girlfriend in *The Hustler*, get ready to be surprised. Her Dolly Talbo is childlike yet profoundly wise, a pagan (as one character calls her) and yet saintly in her love for those who hurt her. For Laurie, this was the role of a lifetime, and she belted it out of the park. I hear that she gave a stunning stage performance as Laura in *The Glass Menagerie* a long time ago, and I believe it, because this is one very talented actress.

Sissy Spacek plays the thankless role of Verena, a hard-edged businesswoman who rules the household but secretly envies Dolly. Walter Matthau plays Charlie Cool with proper restraint (no doubt imposed by his son, who directed). Jack Lemmon, in one of his last roles, plays the con man from Chicago, and Mary Steenburgen is an itinerant evangelist called Sister Ida.

The musical version opened in 1971 and died a quick death. The songs, by Claire Richardson and Ken Elmslie, have been preserved on an original cast recording, and it is one of those "lost musicals" that have earned cult status. No wonder: The cast includes Barbara Cook as Dolly, Karen Morrow (who should have been a big Broadway star but was trapped in failed musicals) as the evangelist called Babylove, and Carol Brice as Catherine. These three fabulous voices help make the recording a keeper. Morrow's show-stopping "The

Babylove Miracle Show" (over 12 minutes long!) makes one realize how miscast Steenburgen was in the movie. And the quality and inventiveness of the music makes one wonder why Richardson didn't become a successful Broadway composer.

Some critics put down Truman Capote as second-rate Tennessee Williams, but in my book Williams is second-rate Capote. You may appreciate Capote for his *Breakfast at Tiffany's*, which seems to be on everyone's list of favorite movies. Quite so; who can forget Audrey Hepburn as Holly Golightly? Not I, certainly. But now that I have seen "The Grass Harp," I will add Piper Laurie's Dolly Talbo to my list of unforgettables.

War Stories

Watching the Ken Burns documentary *The War* last night, I found myself wondering whether I was watching a pro-war or anti-war program. Anti-war, I decided, remembering the images of the dead and wounded soldiers and of the atomized cities of Hiroshima and Nagasaki. One of the veterans of that war, interviewed in the film, had second thoughts about the use of the A-bomb. "Well, I know they say that by killing a quarter million Japanese we might have saved the lives of half a million of our guys, but still....."

As it happened, I switched to *The War* just after watching *Brothers and Strangers*, a British miniseries based on the C.P. Snow novel, in which a team of British scientists, racing to develop their own A-bomb in 1944, are wracked by worries that politicians might turn their work into a weapon of mass annihilation. But they convince themselves that a "demo" of the bomb, in some remote place, would be enough to bring an end to the war. "Surely," one of the scientists says, "No one would be mad enough to actually use the thing."

Anti-war movies are in vogue nowadays, and this fall will bring several new ones. In fact, any honest depiction of war and its consequences has to be anti-war, because war is so vile. Gone are the days when William Bendix and Dane Clark and George Tobias would crack jokes while throwing grenades into enemy trenches or firing machine guns in a B-17 turret. Bendix the Brooklynite, Clark the Italian, Tobias the cigar-smoking Pole, hell-raising heroes all, with the war just a handy backdrop for male bonding.

That was during WW2, of course, when propaganda was in demand. Later movies, like *Twelve O'Clock High*, *The Bridges at Toko-Ri*, and *The Longest Day*, were more believable. But the message was the same: war, though difficult, is essentially a noble endeavor fought by good men (ours). Even *Saving Private Ryan*, much praised for its realism, was in the same mold. *Toko-Ri* came close to the edge by allowing its hero, Brubacher (William Holden) to die a meaningless death in a Korean rice paddy, but then it recanted, as the Admiral (Frederick March) says, with reverential awe, "Where do we get such men?"

Action movies need heroes, and soldiers, sailors, and airmen make great heroes. But for chapter and verse on war heroes, there is no better authority than Lt. Commander Charles Madison (James Garner) in *The Americanization of Emily*. Madison gives his take on war and heroes in the following lines, delivered to Emily (Julie Andrews) and her mother (Joyce Grenfell) in one of the film's many memorable scenes:

Charlie: I don't trust people who make bitter reflections about war, Mrs. Barham. It's always the generals with the bloodiest records who are the first to shout what a Hell it is. And it's always the widows who lead the Memorial Day parades ... we shall never end wars, Mrs. Barham, by blaming it on ministers and generals or warmongering imperialists or all the other banal bogies. It's the rest of us who build statues to those generals and name boulevards after those ministers, the rest of us who make heroes of our dead and shrines of our battlefields. We wear our widows' weeds like nuns and perpetuate war by exalting its sacrifices. My brother died at Anzio – an everyday soldier's death, no special heroism involved. They buried what pieces they found of him. But my mother insists he died a brave death and pretends to be very proud.

Mrs. Barham: You're very hard on your mother. It

seems a harmless enough pretense to me.

Charlie: No, Mrs. Barham. No, you see, now my other brother can't wait to reach enlistment age. That'll be in September. It may be ministers and generals who blunder us into wars, but the least the rest of us can do is to resist honoring the institution. What has my mother got for pretending bravery was admirable? She's under constant sedation and terrified she may wake up one morning and find her last son has run off to be brave.

(For this we are indebted to scriptwriter Paddy Chayefsky, by the way. In the novel, by William Bradford Huie, there is hardly a trace of it. In fact, you will not find Emily's mother, who is so important to the film, anywhere in the novel.)

Mrs. Palfrey at the Claremont

You just can't beat the British when it comes to insightful, literate, well-acted movies. The latest evidence is a quiet little film called *Mrs Palfrey at the Claremont*. Joan Plowright plays the title role, a widow who decides to settle into a London hotel she has seen advertised in a Scottish magazine. The hotel, whose name is announced by a flickering red neon sign, has obviously seen better days, and Mrs P.'s room is small and drab, with a bathroom "down the hall." But Mrs P. decides to give it a go, and she quickly finds herself the center of attention in the Claremont's dining room, where the long-term guests immediately fasten upon her as a new and interesting ingredient in their mélange. These characters include some of the best old-timers of the British stage and screen, with Anna Massey playing the imperious Mrs Arbuthnot, who reassures Mrs P. that she needn't worry about being old because "you're not allowed to die here."

Mrs Palfrey tries to maintain her dignity without being rude to her inquisitors, but their curiosity is irrepressible. Then, walking along the sidewalk one day, Mrs P. trips and falls, and a young man living in an adjacent basement flat rushes to her rescue and ushers her into his digs to recover over a cup of tea. Overcome by his kindness, Mrs P. invites him to dine with her at the Claremont later in the week, and he accepts. His name is Ludwig, and he is an aspiring writer.

Mrs P. has a grandson, Desmond, in London, a fact that the other Claremont guests have pried out of her. But Desmond has not answered her phone calls; he is apparently too busy with his work. So, when Ludwig finally visits and enters the Claremont's dining room, the other guests take him to be Mrs P.'s grandson, and she does not bother to correct them. Later, when the real Desmond and his mother (Mrs P.'s daughter) enter the action, the plot thickens.

But the treasure here is not the plot (based on an Elizabeth Taylor novel), but the characterizations and especially the dialogue. Ludwig's literary ambition sets up references to Wordsworth and Blake and conversations about Mrs P.'s favorite movie (*Brief Encounter*) and song ("For All We Know"). Joan Plowright is perfect in her role, and the supporting cast is nearly as good. We should all spend at least one evening with the flavorful characters in the Claremont's dining room.

Great Britain has given us dozens of movies of this quality, and most of them, like this one, come and go unnoticed on this side of the Atlantic, while the local cineplexes play the likes of *Evan Almighty* and *Oceans Thirty-Seven* (or whatever) and *Live Free or Die Hard*.

De gustibus; non est disputandum.

The Departed

The South Boston Irish, warts and all, make up the world of Martin Scorcese's *The Departed*. They like to drink and womanize, they go to church a lot, and they are capable of turning on each other suddenly and violently, They live and die fatalistically, as if it's no big deal to kill or be killed, because, as Frank Costello (Jack Nicholson) says, when told someone's old mother is on the way out, "so are we all."

The Southie of *The Departed* is not the Southie my Dad always talked about. His Southie was a place of bonding for life. If you were from Southie, you were the salt of the earth. So said my Dad, and on this subject more than any other, his word could be taken to the bank.

But Martin Scorcese was not making a morality play about South Boston. He was making a cops and robbers entertainment, the kind of movie that used to pair Jimmy Cagney and Pat O'Brien, and in this he succeeded brilliantly. Few movies that run for 2-1/2 hours can keep you from looking at your watch along the way (or falling asleep), but in this case the challenge is to keep from falling off the edge of your chair. Two young men, acted to the hilt by Matt Damon and Leonardo diCaprio, play two moles – one working inside the State Police for crime boss Costello, the other working for the police inside the Costello gang. As Costello and the police try to identify the rats in their midst, the tension rises, and by the end, almost every actor playing a central character in *The Departed* turns out to be playing the title role.

Most of the film was shot in Boston, very authentically. The three-deckers, the corner groceries, the hahbah, City Hall, the State House, the subway, the Central Ahtery, all are there. All that was missing was a scene shot at Fenway Pahk or the Boston Gahden. Two of the key actors, Matt Damon and Mark Wahlberg, are native Bostonians, which helps. These and the other members of the excellent cast are all clones of the characters I ran across every day while spending the first 25 years of my life in Boston. Even their names – Billy Costigan, Frank Costello, Colin Sullivan – sounded eerily familiar.

A few days after watching the movie, Jill and I were driving through Norwood, just south of Boston, when we noticed a funeral gathering by the big Catholic church in the center, St. Catherine's. The crowd waiting outside the church was mostly made up of young men, sad-faced and splendid in their black suits.

"I wonder who died," I said as we drove by. Jill, sizing up the scene, figured it out on the spot.

"Billy Costigan."

It is a bloody, extremely violent film, in which the only adjectives permitted are four-letter words and their derivatives. The few women in the story exist only as playthings for the men. But the characters in this world act and talk like that. You will not like most of them, but that's beside the author's point.

The Departed won the Oscar as Best Picture, and I can't argue with that. Of the nominees, I saw *The Queen* (excellent) and *Little Miss Sunshine* (good, but overpraised). In that small sample, *The Departed* stood out for its script, ensemble acting, and direction (another Oscar, for Scorcese). I plan to see *The Last King of Scotland*, another essentially unsavory story about evil men doing evil deeds. From what I have read, Idi Amin and Frank Costello were cut from the same cloth.

The Lost City

A ndy Garcia, I am told, has a checkered reputation among the Hollywood cognoscenti. I don't know anything about that, and I frankly don't care. What I do know is that his movie *The Lost City* shows a great deal of artistry, technical skill, and dedication. It is, in fact, a very good movie – not without flaws, which I will come to, but definitely worth watching.

The story is laid in Havana, just before and after Fidel Castro came to power. Garcia was born in Cuba, and in 1961, two years after the revolution, he and his family fled the island for good. Andy was six at the time. Once he became an established movie actor (in *The Godfather)* with connections, he began nurturing a vision of a movie dealing with the events of the Cuban revolution, set against the sights and sounds (especially the music) of his native land. The movie was released in 2005, and it passed unnoticed. The DVD is available, and that's how I came upon it.

At the center of the story is a Law Professor at Havana University, his wife, and his three sons. The two younger sons are idealists being drawn into the Castro movement. The oldest son, Federico (called Fico), strives to remain apolitical as he runs a Havana cabaret (thus the music). Fico wants nothing more than to keep the family together, but in this he is thwarted by the winds of change. The seizure of the palace and the flight of the dictator Batista are recreated believably, and the suffocating rule of the new regime is also on display. ("Remember," lectures Che Guevara at one point, "the end justifies the means.")

Garcia's direction and his strong portrayal of Fico are impressive. The film has an epic look about it, with gorgeous cinematography (shot in the Dominican Republic) and authentic Cuban music, well performed. The actors playing Fico's parents and his brothers are excellent, as is the Spanish actress Ines Sastre, who provides the love interest. The script, by Cabrera Infante, is intelligent and moving.

So what's not to like?

Garcia apparently could not resist the opportunity to cast two "names" in supporting roles. Bill Murray plays a has-been comedian who attaches himself to Fico and his cabaret, for reasons that are left unexplained. He adds nothing to the story or to the movie. Dustin Hoffman plays the mob leader Meyer Lansky. It's a small part, and 100 other actors could have done it as well. Worse, it is clear in the "making of" feature that Garcia indulged Murray and Hoffman inexcusably, allowing them to insert contrived business and lines. Hoffman is tolerable (barely), Murray is not – although it is clear that Garcia thinks he pulled off a coup in hiring his Pebble Beach golf buddy.

The other failing is the film's length. At the two-hour mark, Fico is flying out of Havana, escaping to New York and a new life, leaving the girlfriend and his parents behind. It is a bittersweet moment, and it is also a perfect closing scene. But no. The story line follows Fico to New York, for 20 more minutes of anticlimactic scenes, some with the extra baggage of Bill Murray and Dustin Hoffman.

Think about the ending of *Casablanca*. Ingrid Bergman and Paul Henreid take off in the plane for Lisbon, while Humphrey Bogart and Claude Rains launch a beautiful friendship. Curtain. Would it have made sense to follow the fugitive couple to Lisbon and watch them set up housekeeping? I don't think so.

These criticisms aside, *The Lost City* is a movie you will not forget. In fact, it could assume cult status at some point, and in post-Castro Cuba it could become a must-see for all those interested in their country's history.

And why did the movie fail to attract much attraction when it was released? Alas, it quickly became entangled in politics. Some South American governments reportedly banned it because they thought it showed Che in a bad light. It was stiffed by some film festivals, and many defenders of Castro attacked it. As I watched it, it seemed to me that both Batista and Castro were vilified, but apparently a right-wing dictator is fair game, a left-wing dictator is not.

Immortal Lines

Movie plots and movie scripts often follow familiar patterns. The standard genres – backstage drama, war saga, sci-fi, crime, romantic comedy, etc. – offer only so many ways to create and resolve tension. The situations are so familiar that one doesn't need to describe them. A line or two of dialogue will bring the whole scene (and possibly the whole movie) into focus. Here are a few examples:

Gee Willikers, Mr. Anderson, Nancy and I were just walking in the field, and a bad thunderstorm came up, and the only place we could go was the old barn. And it kept raining all night. Honest!

I tell you the man came at me with a knife! Why doesn't anyone believe me? George, you're my husband, don't you believe me?

Villiam, my son, I haf been your music teacher for 10 years. You haf great talent. You should be playing Brahms, Schubert, Liszt – not throwing your life avay on this – vat do you call it – chazz?

Yes, Dr. Williams, I am my father's assistant in the laboratory. But don't underestimate me because I'm a woman. I have a doctorate in biothermalnucleogenetic physics.

Carter, my name is Sherman Billingham, the Broadway producer. I caught your act, and I have a spot for you in our new show. But I need only one dancer, not a doubles act. It's your big chance, but I'm afraid you'll have to leave the girl behind.

Look you're the district attorney, and I think you should know there's corruption in the police force, and I think it goes to the very top, maybe even to the commissioner, or higher. All I need is a few more days and I'll break this case wide open. Can I count on your support?

These were brave men, colonel, men who volunteered knowing they'd never come back. Their names will live forever in Marine Corps history: Smith, Scalponetti, Callahan, Shapiro, LeBreque, Kreuger, and Sitkowski.

Honey, I know how much you want to settle down and raise a family, and I promise you that after this one show I'll give it all up.

Phyllis, I have to go to the lab to check out some data on cockroach mutation. I'll be right back. But keep the door locked and don't under any circumstances let anyone in!

The Emperor's Club

Private boys' schools seem to make excellent settings for thoughtful dramas. *Goodbye Mr. Chips, The Browning Version* and *The Winslow Boy* were all excellent examples (although the last of these was centered not on the school scene but on one student's family). A few years back, *Dead Poets Society* was highly popular, and more recently *The History Boys* was a sensation on the stage, with the cast repeating its success on the screen. Most of these dramas are centered on a highly principled, dedicated teacher who endures indifferent (and sometimes scornful) pupils, patronizing superiors, and, in *The Browning Version*, a disloyal wife, to triumph at the end, as the world finally recognizes his true worth.

A fairly recent addition to the genre is *The Emperor's Club*, starring Kevin Kline as William Hundert, a classics scholar and teacher at St. Benedict's School, where the major annual event is not the big football game but the Mr. Julius Caesar competition, in which the three top-ranked classics students, garbed in togas, answer questions about the Roman Republic and Empire, put to them by a moderator. It is an elimination contest, held before the entire student body and invited parents, and Mr. Hundert is Alex Trebek. The winner will be crowned with a Roman garland and immortalized on a school plaque.

Into this scene of erudition and genteel rivalry steps a new student, Sedgewick Bell, a wise guy and goof-off, and a corrupting influence on his classmates. Bell obviously should be thrown out of St. Benedict's posthaste, but that is not an option, for Bell's father is a figure of some importance. In fact, he is the senior U.S. senator from West Virginia. So Sedgewick Bell is tolerated, and Mr. Hundert even starts to nurture illusions about the satisfaction to be gained from the redemption of Sedgewick Bell – even to the point of inflating some marks to allow Bell to qualify for the Mr. Julius Caesar competition.

By now you think you know where this is heading. Young rebel Mickey Rooney being reformed by Father Flanagan in *Boys' Town*, right? Well, no. And here I must leave you guessing, because if you should see the movie you deserve your own surprises. I will say that the plot jumps 25 years to show what becomes of Sedgewick Bell – and to set up one final encounter between the teacher and his old students, as the three 1976 finalists are brought together for a reprise of the Mr. Julius Caesar competition.

It is by no means an unflawed movie. Of its type, it does not compare to *The Browning Version* or *Goodbye Mr. Chips*. On the other hand, I enjoyed it more than I enjoyed *Dead Poets Society*, because its conflicts were more cerebral and less melodramatic. The casting is excellent, particularly in the pairing of the young boys and the men they would become. Emile Hirsch is perfect as the young Sedgewick Bell, and Joel Gretsch is totally believable as the man Sedgewick would become. Kevin Kline has never been better. He gives a laid-back, meditative reading of William Hundert, which I found much more agreeable than the wired performance of Robin Williams in DPS.

Full disclosure: I went to an all-boys high school, where the curriculum was heavy with Latin and Greek. So the subject matter does resonate. But this movie does make an important, even courageous, statement about a value system that seems to celebrate mediocrity. In this year of wall-to-wall political campaigning, it is a message worth considering.

The Oscars

The Academy Awards show has long been a platform for political messages. Most of us, I think, would rather that actors leave the politicking to politicians, but this year the distinction was blurred by the multiple roles of Al Gore as (1) the ranking Democrat on hand, (2) an Oscar winner, for *An Inconvenient Truth*, (3) an advocate for tougher emission standards for the automobile industry, etc. and (4) the credited inspiration for several other Oscar winners, including the best-song winner, Melissa Etheridge. (You may well ask, "What is a song doing in a documentary on global warming anyway?")

But that's okay. By now we all have built-in filters that let us ignore all the sidebars except the host's monologue and the ladies' dresses. These filters block most of the commercials, the awards for short subjects and sound mixing, and the interminable lists of producers. But we can't ignore the incompetence of those Oscar winners who have trouble composing a coherent acceptance speech. Think of it: Here are people who have known for weeks or months that they were nominated, who make their livings memorizing scripted lines, and suddenly they have to pull out a folded piece of paper and then trip all over themselves trying to deliver four or five sentences.

The show's audience is always worth a look, especially the celebrities who rate the choice aisle seats. (It would be fun to eavesdrop on the meetings where such things are decided.) But, filtering aside, it's a classy event, an occasion at which the film industry shows respect for its craft and its craftsmen – as should we all, for, notwithstanding computers and iPods, movies remain our dominant entertainment medium.

For me, the appetizer for this year's Oscar show was Christopher Guest's latest movie, *For Your Consideration*, which describes the effect on the cast of a low-budget movie (*Home for Purim*) when one of the actors is rumored to be under consideration for an Oscar nomination. The Christopher Guest troupe, so hilarious in *Waiting for Guffman* and *Best in Show*, is back. Unfortunately, the spirit that made those two movies so special is missing. Catherine O'Hara is fine as the subject of the rumor, as are Jennifer Coolidge as a clueless producer and Eugene Levy as a slimy agent, but the whole thing just doesn't come off, possibly because Guest departed from his successful mockumentary format, possibly because the gang's improv skills have been tapped out and it is time for a good script. There are enough choice moments in the film to make it worth watching, but Guest's fans will be disappointed.

We should not leave the Oscars without commenting on this year's host. Ellen DeGeneres was adequate. That's not a knock; several hosts in recent years have been less than adequate. My own favorites were Steve Martin and Billy Crystal. Crystal seemed poised for a long run, but long runs – like that of Bert Parks in the Miss America pageant – are apparently not in the cards. Or maybe the Academy thinks Miss DeGeneres can build a following. Off this year's performance, she deserves another shot.

Also making it through our filter is the annual filmed tribute to those movie greats who died since the last Awards show. The list seems to get longer with each year, which I suppose is only natural, but this year served up a bumper crop, including Glenn Ford, June Allyson, Jack Warden, Don Knotts, Jack Palance, Jane Wyman, and Alida Valli. They gave us many hours of entertainment and in fact still do.

Snow Cake

Alex Hughes had a fling with a girl named Rebecca a long time ago. A son was born of that fling, a son Alex never knew about. Then, years later, he found out, and he arranged to meet his son for dinner at a restaurant in London. Alex had never married, and there would probably be no other children, so he waited for his only child with great anticipation. But his son never came. He was killed by a motorist while crossing the street. An enraged Alex found the driver, hit him, and knocked him down. The motorist died, and Alex was sentenced to several years in prison for manslaughter. He served his time and was released, but the totality of the experience leaves him a desolate man, with little to live for.

Desperate for closure, Alex searches for Rebecca and finds that she is living in Winnipeg. So he sets out for Winnipeg, not by the most direct route, but by flying to Toronto and setting out overland for Manitoba.

This is the back story. You will find it out, piecemeal, but I am not spoiling the story by telling you that much. The movie is called *Snow Cake*. It was made in 2006. It was written by Angela Pell and directed by Marc Evans.

Snow Cake is an engrossing, well written, brilliantly acted story about what happens to Alex Hughes on the way to Manitoba. To tell you more would involve a spoiler, and this is a story best appreciated when you don't know what's coming next.

The leading roles are played by Alan Rickman and Sigourney Weaver. Emily Hampshire is memorable in a key supporting role. The movie cost petty cash to make and was filmed in about a month. In the era of mega-movies, *Snow Cake* reminds us that a good story, well acted and well written, need not cost a fortune. The corollary is that a $100 million movie without a good story well told can be a turkey. Some years ago, as we left the theater after seeing *Titanic*, Jill summed it up thus: "There were 1500 people on that ship, and they couldn't find a story better than that?"

Two Hugo Movies

I saw two Hugo movies in the last few days. One was *Les Miserables,* the musical based on Victor Hugo's classic novel. The other was Martin Scorsese's *Hugo*, a fantasy based on Brian Selznick's children's book. Both were terrific.

Les Miserables

Les Miserables, popularly called *Les Miz*, is one of the most successful musical-theater productions of all time, and its transfer to the big screen has been eagerly awaited. The wait was worth it. Hugh Jackman, as the hero Jean Valjean, is simply marvelous. The Australian is of course no stranger to the musical theater, but his past successes do not prepare you for his performance in *Les Miz*. He is a certain contender (if there is any justice) for a best actor Oscar.

One of the best roles the musical theater has to offer is that of Jean Valjean's stalker, the policeman Javert, and once again Hollywood chose box-office appeal rather than talent. Not that Russell Crowe can't act; he is in fact an excellent actor, but he is no singer, so Javert's dramatic soliloquy *Stars* does not get the show-stopping treatment it deserves. It is an exasperating miss, reminiscent of Hollywood's choice of Rosalind Russell over Ethel Merman in *Gypsy* or its snub of Julie Andrews in *My Fair Lady*.

Anne Hathaway, not known as a singer, handles her songs very well, and her acting has earned her widespread praise. Amanda Seyfried plays Cosette rather woodenly. Speaking of wood, Helena Bonham Carter plays Madame Thenardier. Her husband, the "master of the house," is played adequately by Sacha Baron Cohen.

The real star, aside from Hugh Jackman, is the material. The book is incredibly good, and the score is stunning. (The same composer gave us *Miss Saigon,* whose score is almost as good.) Bottom line: Despite the shortcomings, this motion picture is well worth seeing.

Hugo

In my opinion, *Hugo* is Martin Scorsese's masterpiece. This is the tale of a young boy (Hugo) who tends the big clock in a Paris railroad station, after the deaths of his father, a mechanical whiz, and his uncle, a drunkard. Hugo lives in the dark recesses of the station, where he must avoid the clutches of the gendarme (Sacha Baron Cohen), who sweeps boys like Hugo into the orphanage. Hugo, who has inherited his father's love of machinery, works on an automaton left by his father – an automaton, Hugo believes, which holds an important message.

In the station is a toy shop, whose owner is a misanthrope (Ben Kingsley) who, it turns out, once was a movie pioneer. There are thus two story threads, one involving the boy and his automaton, one involving the earliest days of movies, and the two threads merge in a conclusion that is wholly satisfying. The movie is, in a word, wonderful. The recreation of 1930's Paris is staggeringly beautiful. (One can see why the film cost $170 million to produce.) The acting is topnotch, as are the cinematography, the music, and, most of all, the charming story. A plus: It is a film that families can enjoy together. Now, how many Martin Scorsese movies can you say that about?

Moneyball

A long with the mediocrity from Hollywood these days, there is the rare movie written and directed for thinking adults. Such a film is *Moneyball*, starring Brad Pitt, written by Steven Zaillian and Aaron Sorkin, and directed by Bennett Miller. They deserve all the awards they can pick up. *Moneyball* tells the story of the 2002 Oakland Athletics, a small-market baseball team that must find a way to be competitive against the American League goliaths, New York and Boston.

General Manager Billy Beane (Brad Pitt) decides that the key lies in statistics, as massaged by a young Yale economics graduate (Jonah Hill). And the new system that Beane crafts works. The Athletics have a fine season, along the way breaking the baseball record for consecutive wins. Of course, there is always resistance to change, especially in a tradition-bound game like baseball, and the tension between the old guard and the young rebels gives the film its edge. But the film is notable, not only for what it includes, but for what it does not. There is not a single steamy scene. Robin Wright, as Beane's ex-wife, shows up for a few seconds and appears on the posters, but anyone who is drawn to the movie by her presence is going to be disappointed, for her character could as easily have been played by the check-out girl at your local Wal-Mart. And there is no violence, save for a few of Billy Beane's temper tantrums, which are brief and don't really count.

What gives *Moneyball* its flavor is the honest portrayal of the characters in the front office, the back office, and all the offices in between. And "characters" is the word. It gives us a picture of the machinery of baseball that is lacking in any other baseball movie, including my ex-favorite, *Bull Durham*. (Sorry about that, Crash.) *Moneyball* is a feel-good movie. Well, maybe feel-better, since the Oakland team didn't win the World Series or even the pennant in 2002. But that, in an odd way, is one of film's strengths. If Billy Beane's bunch of misfits had won it all, that would have been too Hollywood.

Inside baseball: Paul DePodesta, the young nerd played (under a different name) by Jonah Hill, is now VP for Player Development with the Mets. He also looks more like a movie star than a nerd, but the producer must have thought that one handsome guy was quite enough. (The producer was Brad Pitt.) Anyway, Jonah Hill is perfect in the role, providing a nice roly-poly contrast with the trim Pitt. Columbia, which had first dibs on the film, bowed out in protest over script revisions.)

I don't know how many Oscars *Moneyball* will win. Maybe none. Maybe, like the 2002 Athletics, it will have to be satisfied with having a good run. That counts in my book.

Postcards from the Edge

To judge by its subject matter, *Postcards from the Edge* is a movie I would not watch. But there it was on the telly, and before I could change the channel I caught a bit of dialogue that sounded clever. And then another bit of bright dialogue, and then a whole scene, and I was hooked. That was about 10 years ago. The other night I watched it again to see if my first impressions deceived me. They did not. It's a very good movie.

If you haven't seen it, it's a story about a mother-daughter relationship, written by Carrie Fisher, an authority on the subject. The mother, played by Shirley MacLaine, is an alcoholic. The daughter, played by Meryl Streep, is a junkie. Three things elevate the film above its story line: (1) Meryl Streep, (2) Shirley Maclaine, and (3) the wisdom of Carrie Fisher's writing.

The movie takes place in Hollywood, for the mother is an over-the-hill movie actress and the daughter is trying to climb the hill. Say, doesn't that sound like Debbie Reynolds and Carrie Fisher? No, but close. Carrie carries around lots of bittersweet memories about Mom and Eddie Fisher, her dad, who left Debbie for Elizabeth Taylor, who left Eddie for Richard Burton, who left...... Some of the memories undoubtedly "informed" *Postcards*, but Carrie was saving the best stuff for her one-woman show, *Wishful Drinking*, shown on HBO.

In *Postcards*, Mom advises daughter that she should give up acting in third-rate movies and focus instead on a singing career. The advice is sound, but the daughter is wary: Mom sings, and she doesn't want to compete with Mom, because Mom always wins. Interesting sidelight: A review of *Wishful Drinking* notes that Carrie Fisher is a talented singer, though Mom is of course the "name" singer. (Personal note: As an emcee at an industry conference, I once shared a stage with Debbie Reynolds and found her great fun to work with. It is hard for me to believe that Shirley MacLaine was accurately channeling Debbie, but of course I don't know.)

The scenes between Streep and MacLaine are the core of this movie. They are duels dripping with bitterness, and they are terrific. Others flit around the edges of the story: Gene Hackman is just right as a film director, and Richard Dreyfuss, Rob Reiner, and Dennis Quaid help out in roles that are inconsequential.

It was no surprise to find Meryl Streep delivering another solid performance. But MacLaine outdid herself. She is best known as a talented singer and dancer, but here was a dramatic turn that was very demanding, and she scored a bull's eye. At least some of the credit for her bitchy performance must go to Director Mike Nichols, who also directed *Who's Afraid of Virginia Woolf*, with Elizabeth Taylor as the bitchy Martha.

Hollywood is a very small world.

The Americanization of Emily

J ulie Andrews says that of all the movies she's made, *The Americanization of Emily* is her favorite. So says James Garner, her co-star. So says Arthur Hiller, who directed. Why has this movie, released in 1964, captivated so many people ?

There are many reasons, but at the top of the list must be the literary, highly pungent script of Paddy Chayefsky. Producer Martin Ransohoff spotted the William Bradford Huie novel, which tells of a romance between an Admiral's aide (the dust cover says it's "the further adventures of Lieutenant-Commander James Monroe Madison of *The Revolt of Mamie Stover*") and a British woman in WW2 London, and Ransohoff optioned it, thinking it might make a pleasant enough romantic comedy. In time, William Holden was penciled in as the hero, James Garner was to play Madison's sidekick, and William Wyler was chosen as the movie's director.

Then Wyler and Holden pulled out, Arthur Hiller was named director, Garner was given the lead, and, most importantly, Paddy Chayefsky was asked to write the screenplay. And what a screenplay he created! The book is a routine love story, with the D-Day invasion the only memorable action. Commander Madison is a writer whose skills as a procurer (of booze and broads, mostly) for Navy brass have landed him in the lap of luxury in London. Emily Barham is a volunteer driver attached to Madison's unit. Madison and Barham fall in love and, after he makes a movie of the D-Day landing, live happily and peacefully ever after.

Enter Paddy Chayefsky. He is not interested in telling a typical Doris Day/Rock Hudson romantic comedy. In his hands, Commander Madison is a practicing coward, whose overriding ambition is not to get killed in the war, and whose service as a valued "dog-robber" seems to guarantee survival. Emily Barham, who has lost a father, a husband, and a brother to war, is a Yank-hating moralist, who buys into the nobility of a hero's death.

This is all Chayefsky. In the book, Madison is as patriotic as the next man, and when the Admiral orders him to film the invasion, he gets a camera crew and obediently joins the fleet.

In the movie, Chayefsky writes a sparkling scene in which Madison and Emily's mother spar over the reality of war and the folly of glamorizing it. Madison expresses his philosophy of life, sacrifice, and honor, and he makes his pursuit of survival sound almost noble. It is an indispensable scene – and yet, in the book, there is not a word of dialogue about these subjects.

One shouldn't be too hard on the book's author. He was simply writing a different story. Yet if the screenplay followed the book's outline, the movie would have been forgotten long ago.

Arthur Hiller was a rookie Hollywood director in 1963,

when he began shooting *Emily*. He would later direct some good movies, like *The In-Laws, The Hospital*, and *Plaza Suite*, but nothing, in his mind, to compare with *Emily*. Julie Andrews, of course, is everybody's sweetheart no matter what she does, but she, too, singles out this movie as her best. And James Garner is an absolutely perfect Charlie Madison. The rest of the cast is solid: Joyce Grenfell as the dotty mother, Melvyn Douglas as the Admiral, and James Coburn as Bus. There is practically no music in the film other than the song *Emily*, heard over the credits.

Hard as it is to believe, *The Americanization of Emily* was made almost a half century ago. But it is still immensely enjoyable, and Paddy Chayefsky's message still makes sense today.

The Last Station

The Last Station is a little-known movie about the last year or so of Tolstoy's life, starring Christopher Plummer as Tolstoy and Helen Mirren as his wife Sonya. It is also a clinic in the acting art by two of the finest professionals in the field.

The conflict that animates the drama is the question of who will own the rights to Tolstoy's work when he dies. Tolstoy and his legions of followers do not believe in private property. As they see it, the public at large is the rightful inheritor of his creative output. His wife Sonya just as strongly believes that Tolstoy's primary obligation is to provide for the welfare of his family. A standoff? No, because of the powerful influence of Chertkov, a leader of the Tolstoy movement and a confidante of the master, played brilliantly by Paul Giamatti. The title of the film refers to the station on the railroad line where Tolstoy spends his last days.

The facts as portrayed by the film are as accurate as one should expect of a movie (I checked it against Henri Troyat's biography). But the grabber here is not authenticity but the power of the acting. Plummer *is* Tolstoy. Mirren *is* Sonya. (Did you know that Helen Mirren was born Ilyena Lydia Vasilievna Mironoff?)

As so often happens, my enthusiasm for the film led me to seek out Christopher Plummer's memoir, *In Spite of Myself*. It is a long book, and there is no evidence that anyone collaborated with him in the writing. Plummer, Canadian by birth, is now 81 years old, so one must be impressed by his energy if nothing else. But the writing quality is excellent, revealing a sharp memory and wit.

The title of the book, I guess, refers to the fact that he has lived a successful life in spite of the fact that he was generally irresponsible, a drinker, a womanizer, and an ingrate. He rather cheerfully admits all this, and the gallery of the rich and famous people whose lives intersect with his makes the book endlessly fascinating.

Harry Warren

The other night I watched one of those collections of musical numbers from past Tony Award Shows, and the opening sequence bowled me over – again. It was the ultimate tap-dancing spectacle, the title number from *42d Street*. Here in one magical scene is an encapsulation of everything that persuades so many of us that the Broadway musical is *the* art form of our age. The tap dancers then segued into "We're in the Money" from the same show. More magic. More proof, I thought, of the genius of Harry Warren.

It seems that every year brings a new tribute to George Gershwin, and another to Irving Berlin. We have also seen specials featuring the music of Cole Porter, Andrew Lloyd-Webber, and Jerry Herman. The music of Richard Rodgers has been lavishly (and justly) celebrated, as have the works of his collaborators Hart and Hammerstein. All this is as it should be; at least three-quarters of all the popular songs we now regard as standards came from these and a mere handful of other composers.

But there have been no television specials, none that I'm aware of anyway, about the man who may have been the most successful hit-song composer of them all, with the exception of Berlin. His name was Harry Warren.

Here's a sample of the Warren songbook:

You're My Everything
Shuffle Off to Buffalo
You're Getting to be a Habit With Me
Forty-Second Street
I Only Have Eyes For You
We're in the Money
Lullaby of Broadway
The Atchison, Topeka, and the Santa Fe
September in the Rain
There Will Never Be Another You
I Had the Craziest Dream
Remember Me
The More I See You
The Shadow Waltz
This Heart of Mine
You Must Have Been a Beautiful Baby
About a Quarter to Nine
Serenade in Blue
You'll Never Know
Chattanooga Choo Choo
That's Amore

Between 1935 and 1950, the yardstick of music popularity was a weekly radio show called *Your Hit Parade*, which featured the 10 most often played songs. Over that 15-year span, 42 Harry Warren songs made the list. Berlin was second, with 33. Yet, while everyone has heard of Berlin, Harry Warren is a relative unknown. Why?

One answer is that he wrote his songs almost exclusively for the movies, not for Broadway. The movies he wrote for were mostly forgettable, but his songs were too good to be forgotten. Take, for instance, a 1942 flick called *Iceland*, starring Sonja Henie. It is completely and rightly forgotten, but the beautiful "There Will Never Be Another You," written by Warren for this film, is still alive and well, a standard by any measure.

Another handicap for Warren was his retiring nature. While some composers, including Porter, Gershwin, and Berlin, were personalities in their own right, Warren shied away from celebrity. At the Academy Award banquet in 1936, where Warren won an Oscar for "Lullaby of Broadway," he had trouble getting by the door guard, who didn't know who he was.

Warren worked as a contract songwriter at Warner Brothers and Twentieth Century Fox for much of his career, but eventually he, like most of the top-tier musical talent of the day, was scooped up by MGM and its legendary Freed unit.

His first MGM musical was *The Harvey Girls*, for which he was paired with lyricist Johnny Mercer. The movie (a Judy Garland vehicle) and Warren's score were successful, and the composer picked up another best-song Oscar, for "The Atchison, Topeka, and the Santa Fe."

Harry Warren wrote songs to order, and his songs were the property of the studios to use or not use as they saw fit. Most of his songs were well received, but once in a while a song didn't fit the script. A hauntingly beautiful, minor-key ballad called "There is No Music For Me" was written by Harry Warren and Ira Gershwin for the Astaire-Rogers movie, *The Barkleys of Broadway*. It was cut from the film and never heard until it was unearthed for a TV special (on Gershwin, not Warren, of course).

After his years with MGM, Warren worked for Paramount and Fox, and in the twilight of his career turned out the title song for *An Affair to Remember* – a perfect background for the popular Cary Grant-Deborah Kerr romance. This was a remake of an earlier film called *Love Affair* (with Charles Boyer and Irene Dunne), and the new film and its theme song were to have the same name as the original. But the producers then found that they had bought the rights to the movie - but not to the title. Warren and his lyricist Harold Adamson then had to scramble to turn their new song "Love Affair" into "An Affair to Remember." No one listening to Vic Damone singing the song over the opening credits would ever suspect that the final line "…a love affair to remember" was a last-minute rework.

Warren was born Salvatore Guaragna in 1893, the last of 11 children. He grew up loving opera, especially Puccini, as well as liturgical music at his parish in Brooklyn. Then, in 1915, he started working for

Vitagraph as a bit-part actor. One of the Vitagraph stars, Corrine Griffith, heard him playing the piano, liked what she heard, and soon he was composing and playing music to accompany silent films.

Like Richard Rodgers and Irving Berlin, Harry Warren created memorable songs out of deceptively simple melodies. Take "The More I See You," for instance: A simple five-note theme, then repeated an interval higher; what's so tricky about that? Then the lead-in to the release, four B-flats ("With every sigh") with the harmonic progression moving from B-flat seventh to E-flat minor, and we are in new territory.

"This Heart of Mine" starts innocently enough with its first four notes, then opens up beautifully on its way to a release in which nine straight Cs are harmonized by F, A-flat-seventh, and D-flat chords. This song is given an over-the-top MGM treatment in the movie *Ziegfeld Follies*, with Fred Astaire and Lucille Bremer dancing out a playlet about a jewel thief, but to me the real star is the rich Conrad Salinger orchestration of this gorgeous Harry Warren melody.

Warren finally got a share of the spotlight when the classic old movie *42d Street* was turned into a hit Broadway musical, starring Jerry Orbach. The show opened on Broadway in the fall of 1980. Harry Warren died the following year, but hardly anyone outside show business noticed.

Frank Loesser

T oday's Wall Street Journal brought a long review of a new book about Frank Loesser, and, since my antennae always home in on articles about the great songwriters, I dove into the story expecting enrichment. Instead, I was left wondering how a reviewer, presumably knowledgeable about the subject, could spend 1000 words or so on the musical achievements of Frank Loesser – a giant among American composers – without once mentioning the Loesser masterpiece, *The Most Happy Fella*. Instead, what we got was a lot of gushing about Loesser's pop tunes, "Baby It's Cold Outside," "A Slow Boat to China" and "What Are You Doing New Year's?" Good songs all, but they are mere footnotes in the illustrious biography of Frank Loesser.

To those in the know, Loesser gave Broadway two blockbusters: *Guys and Dolls* and The *Most Happy Fella*, and if he never wrote another musical or another song, that would qualify him for the Pantheon. Yes, *How to Succeed...*" won a Pulitzer, but its score is second rate. He also wrote *Where's Charley?* and *Greenwillow*, but most of his 700 or so songs were written as singles, many of them becoming standards.

But let's return to the two masterpieces. *Guys and Dolls* and *The Most Happy Fella* are so different that it is hard to believe they are the works of the same composer. The opening of *Guys and Dolls* marks the show as an instant classic. Three "guys" sing about their favorite horses in today's race. Nicely-Nicely likes Paul Revere, Benny is betting on Valentine, and Epitaph is Rusty Charlie's choice. The "Fugue for Tinhorns" develops into a contrapuntal trio that sets the tone for the show. In the title song, we learn that "when you see a gent paying all kinds of rent for a flat that would flatten the Taj Mahal," he must be doing it for some doll. Can lyrics get any better than that?

The Most Happy Fella is operatic, with Loesser pouring out one beautiful melody after another – enough for three musicals, really. The story, based on Sidney Howard's play *They Knew What They Wanted*, centers on Tony, a middle-aged, Italian wine grower from the Napa Valley who falls in love with a San Francisco waitress, courts her by mail, and, when it comes time to swap pictures, sends her a photograph of his handsome foreman, Joe. When she travels to Napa and discovers the deception, she is enraged, seeks solace in Joe's arms, and becomes pregnant. But when kind-hearted Tony is injured in an accident, she decides to stay on and take care of him. She falls in love with Tony, Joe packs up and leaves, singing that he's had "all I want of the ladies in the neighborhood." Tony is more than happy at the prospect of serving as the father of Rosabella's baby.

It is a rich, warm love story, whose Napa Valley setting seems to cry out for a Puccini score. And we get it, with no compromise, from Frank Loesser, complete with festival songs ("Abbondanza", "Sposalizio") and dramatic arias ("My Heart is So Full of You," "A Long Time Ago"). But for all its operatic soul, at heart this is a Broadway musical as well, so Loesser gives us "Big D" and "Standing on the Corner."

I saw the Broadway original production in 1956, buying standing room at the sold-out Imperial. And I would do it again, even with my creaky knee. Tony was played by Robert Weede, Rosabella by Jo Sullivan (later Mrs. Frank Loesser). That amazing production was captured – not just the songs, but the whole play – in a three-LP recording, which is one of my most prized possessions. You don't have a turntable? Not to worry: Sony has issued the entire original-cast album on a two-CD set. This is musical theater the likes of which you just don't find anymore, because they aren't making Frank Loessers anymore.

Songs of War

In World War 1, the doughboys marched off to war singing "Over There," "It's a Long Way to Tipperary," "It's a Grand Old Flag," and "Yankee Doodle Dandy." The British and the French, not to be outdone, had their own long list of songs designed to keep spirits high. Irving Berlin pulled "God Bless America" out of his trunk and, with Kate Smith's help, made it a second national anthem. Frank Loesser contributed "Praise the Lord and Pass the Ammunition" and Jule Styne and Sammy Cahn wrote "I'll Walk Alone." From Old Blighty we heard Vera Lynn promise that "We'll Meet Again" and "There'll be Bluebirds Over the White Cliffs of Dover," while a uniformed Irving Berlin was on stage singing how he hated to get up in the morning. There were dozens if not hundreds of songs about soldiers, sailors, marines, and the girls back home, some of them, like Rosie, working away as riveters. The musical legacy of World War 2 lives on, as many of the tunes became standards that are ingrained in the national psyche.

Then things changed. Nobody sang sentimental ballads about the Korean War or about Vietnam. (The musical "Miss Saigon" has many fine songs, but they are mostly bitter or satirical.) We are now engaged in war once again, but nobody's writing songs about it. ("It's a Long Way to Sadr City"? I don't think so.) As a society, we have progressed to the point where no one writes melodies romanticizing war. We are endlessly exhorted to "support our troops" by supporting the latest tactical surge, but even that line is getting tired, and no one is setting it to music.

Of course, hardly anyone is writing romantic ballads of any kind these days, and we are all the poorer for that. A song like "I'll Walk Alone" was really a love song, not a war song, and that is why it is still sung. Most of the true war songs didn't last. They sold War Bonds and made people feel patriotic, but now they are forgotten.

Oh, by the way, the U.S. and its allies didn't hold a monopoly on war songs in WW2. I have a book of Soviet popular songs of that era, and, in case you're curious, here are the lyrics for one of them, "Tachanka," translated into English:

Fly, oh bird, above the highway,
Beast aside, to the clear road.
Look and see the dust roll skyward,
Raised by horses swiftly rode.
Taking aim with his machine gun,
The young gunner opens fire.
And staccato shots unseen zip,
Making all the foes retire.
Eh, Tachanka rostovchanka,
You're a beauty and our pride.
With the mounted troops Tachanka,
On four wheels you swiftly ride.

Well, it probably loses something in translation.

Allegro – The New Recording

Let's turn our attention to weightier matters, like the new recording of Rodgers and Hammerstein's *Allegro*. This musical, following on the heels of *Oklahoma* and *Carousel*, was so eagerly awaited (it had the largest advance sale in history) it just had to disappoint. And disappoint it did, for reasons that people still argue about today. In my opinion it was by far the best of the R&H flops and the one most deserving of another chance. If you would like to learn more about my thoughts on the original *Allegro* (which I saw, incidentally, back in 1947), you'll find it elsewhere in this book.

But today I would like to rave about the new, "first complete recording" of *Allegro*. It is wonderful, thanks to the dedicated efforts of Ted Chapin of the Rodgers and Hammerstein Organization, R&H Music Director Bruce Pohamac, conductor Larry Blank, David Lai of Sony, and a few other colleagues, and a dream cast, including Audra McDonald, Laura Benanti, Nathan Gunn, and Liz Callaway. And a talented group of musicians in Bratislava.

Bratislava? Well, yes, because a Slovakian orchestra was looking for work, schooled in the romantic tradition, and available. So off Chapin and buddies went to Bratislava, where they gave the orchestra the magnificent Robert Russell Bennett orchestrations, rehearsed, and recorded – just the orchestra. Then, the audio tracks safely stowed, they flew back to the U.S., recorded the chorus, then the soloists, then a final recording session to add some neat touches, like the voice of Oscar Hammerstein. When you hear the final product, you will think all 70 cast members and the Istropolis Philharmonic Orchestra were gathered together in a huge recording hall, but you will be wrong, because we are living in the age where little children have learned to ask "Is it *real*, daddy?"

But all the audio razzle-dazzle would have been wasted without sure-fire casting and without one of Rodgers's most melodic scores to work with. Whatever the faults of *Allegro*, the score is not among them. If you are old enough, you may remember "A Fellow Needs a Girl" or "So Far." If you are also tuned in to show music, you may even recall "You Are Never Away" or "The Gentleman is a Dope." But my own favorites are "I Know It Can Happen Again," "Winters Go By," 'Wish Them Well," and "Come Home, Joe," sung by Audra McDonald. Hearing Audra wrap her glorious voice round that one song is worth the cost of the entire two-disc set.

The play tells the story of Joseph Taylor, Jr., son of a country doctor and destined to become a doctor himself. It begins with Junior's birth, follows him through school, medical school, romance, marriage, and his fateful encounter with the decision of his life: whether to climb the medical escalator in the big Chicago hospital or return to join his dad in his home town. This being a Hammerstein book, you'd expect Joe to chuck the high life in favor of the honest labors of the country doctor, and you'd be right - eventually. But, in a most un-Hammerstein twist, the girl he married, his childhood sweetheart, turns out to be seduced by the glitter (and by a wealthy hospital benefactor), and Joe goes home without her – but with nurse Emily, who, it is assumed, will marry him once the legalities are sorted out.

In the original, Emily was played by Lisa Kirk, and a highlight was her "The Gentleman is a Dope." Lisa came off as a sadder but wiser nurse, who knows the score, even though the gentleman doesn't. In the new recording, Emily is sung by Liz Callaway, a much sweeter proposition with a less torchy reading of the lyric. The casting apparently surprised a few people, but the producers asked themselves who would be more likely to leave the big city and follow her fellow back to the sticks – Elaine Stritch or Julie Andrews?

There is a lot of music on these two discs, and it is not, I must say, all gold. A few songs – "Ya-ta-ta," "Money Isn't Everything," and the title song – are clunkers, because their irony places them more in Sondheimland than in the world of R&H. In fact, it is worth noting that Stephen Sondheim was a gofer for the original *Allegro*, just as Ted Chapin was a gofer, much later, for Sondheim's *Follies*.

The few shortcomings aside, the new recording of *Allegro* deserves a place in the collection of anyone who loves Broadway music and musicals. I also have the original cast recording of the show, but I doubt that I'll listen to it any more; the new one seems destined to be, for the foreseeable future, the definitive recording of this fine, underrated musical.

John McGlinn and The Song

John McGlinn was an orchestra conductor and musical archivist. His lifelong passion was a quest for the original orchestrations of musicals, some well known, others long forgotten. He was, in fact, a musical archaeologist, digging through old warehouses and attics in search of history. In 1982, McGlinn made his biggest find in an abandoned warehouse in Seacaucus, NJ – the original orchestrations for *Showboat*, the 1927 Kern-Hammerstein production that arguably was the most significant musical of the twentieth century. "It was like finding Tut's tomb," he said as he remembered the moment.

McGlinn's special mission was to find the original versions of songs written by Jerome Kern, regarded by many as the inventor of the American popular song. Many of Kern's songs were written in collaboration with Oscar Hammerstein II (best known today for his later collaboration with Richard Rodgers). The Kern-Hammerstein partnership produced, in addition to *Showboat*, two other hit shows, *Sunny* and *Music in the Air*. Then, in 1939, the masters gave us *Very Warm for May*, which featured what I believe is the best love song ever written, "All the Things You Are." The original orchestrations for this song were among the treasures that John McGlinn saved from obscurity.

The melody line is harmonically inspired, but it doesn't explain the song's appeal; it's the harmony that raises the goose bumps, and that is why McGlinn's discovery was so important.

The lyrics are Hammerstein at his best. "You are the promised kiss of springtime that makes the lonely winter seem long" may not seem special if you have never spent a lonely winter in Maine, but trust me, it rings the bell, as does "the breathless hush of evening that trembles on the brink of a lovely song." That's the kind of writing that drives would-be writers like me to desperation.

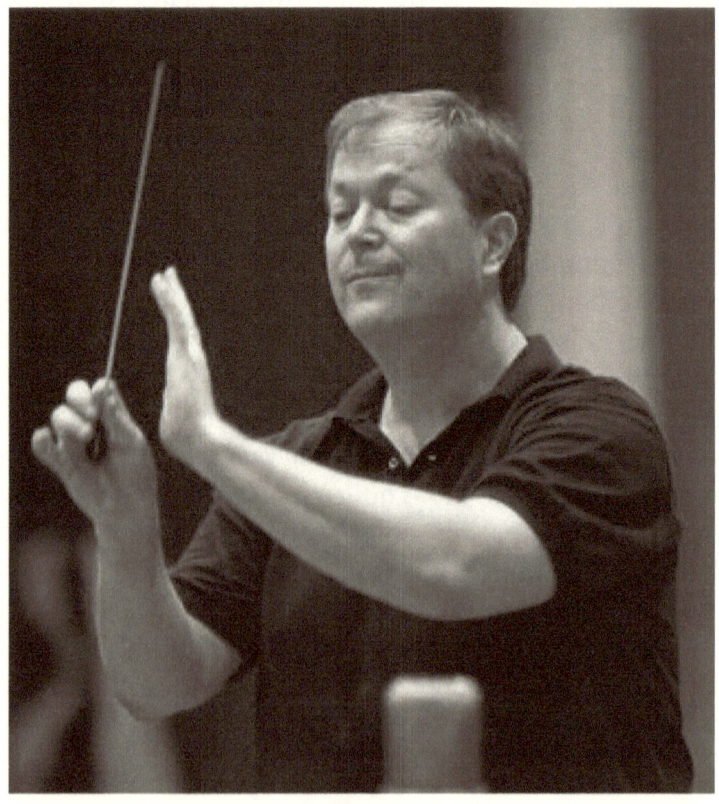

In 1990, the Boston Pops Orchestra devoted an hour to songs from old Broadway shows, and they put that "Evening at the Pops" in the hands of guest conductor John McGlinn, proving that there is justice in the world after all. I taped the program, and I can report that the beatific smile on McGlinn's face as he conducted spoke volumes about his love for these orchestrations, especially the grand finale, the original Russell Bennett orchestration of "All the Things You Are" - just as the opening night audience heard it 50 years before, said hostess Kitty Carlisle-Hart.

The song is a double duet, with one couple singing the verse (rarely heard today), each singer expressing frustration at his/her inability to "let my heart find its voice," followed by the other couple's all-out declaration of love. In the show, the song was sung early in the first act, then reprised twice in the second act, suggesting that the producers knew where the gold lay. In the Pops concert, the two couples were joined by the Tanglewood Chorus. Talk about giving a great song its due!

Very Warm for May, despite a huge cast, lots of talent (June Allyson, Eve Arden, Vera Ellen), and the creative energies of Kern and Hammerstein, lasted only 59 performances. But it did leave behind a song that will live forever.

And John McGlinn must still be smiling – from above. A heart attack took him at age 55.

The Rodgers & Hammerstein Flops (I)

Ome fall afternoon in 1947, I went to the Colonial Theater to see a new Rodgers and Hammerstein musical, in Boston for its pre-Broadway tryout. I paid, as I recall, $1.20 to sit in the second balcony for the matinee. The musical was *Allegro*, the third R&H collaboration. The first two, *Oklahoma!* and *Carousel*, had been huge hits. At the time I had seen neither, but the songs from those shows were all over the radio, and I figured that anybody who could write "You'll Never Walk Alone," "If I Loved You," and "Oh, What a Beautiful Morning" was worth $1.20 and a subway ride downtown. I liked *Allegro* immensely (at 17, I liked everything immensely), but mine was a minority view, and the play, despite a reasonable run and a modest profit, is generally considered a failure. That judgment should be reexamined. Maybe I was right after all.

One strike against *Allegro* was high expectations. After *Oklahoma!* and *Carousel*, the public expected nothing but masterpieces from Rodgers and Hammerstein, and *Allegro* didn't measure up to its predecessors. But it was still an excellent play, with a fine score. There are not as many memorable songs as in *Carousel* (how could there be?), but "A Fellow Needs a Girl" has a warmth characteristic of Rodgers at his best, and "You Are Never Away," is a tune that stays with you. Best of all is "The Gentleman is a Dope." Fifty-nine years later, I can still see Lisa Kirk, alone on the stage, dressed in a raincoat, singing "Why am I crying my eyes out? He doesn't belong to me."

There are other solid musical numbers, including the anthemic "Wish Them Well" and the ballad "So Far," which became fairly popular at the time. The score would have been even stronger had not a song called "My Wife" been cut at the last minute. The melody resurfaced in *South Pacific* as "Younger Than Springtime."

Allegro traces the life of Joseph Taylor, Jr., the son of a small-town doctor and eventually a doctor himself. Under the influence of a grasping young wife, he abandons his friends and family to seek his fortune in the Big City (in this case, Chicago). *Allegro* at its core is a morality play, in which goodness (simple, honest country folk) is pitted against Mammon (rich, selfish city people). Hammerstein, who wrote the book, was roundly accused of preachiness. The librettist himself acknowledged the weakness, in a backhanded way. He didn't mean to portray small-town doctors and city doctors as proxies for good and evil, he explained, but if audiences took it that way, well, he must not have made his points clear enough. Indeed. One critic suggested that, if big cities were that immoral, what was Hammerstein doing in New York, climbing the ladder of success and amassing millions in the process? Maybe he and Rodgers should be spending their time in some community theater in Indiana.

No one hates message plays more than I do, but it seems to me that this criticism of *Allegro* is overdone. The choices confronted by *Allegro*'s hero are legitimate material for a drama, and if the city and country characters are a bit overdrawn, this is far from class warfare. Oscar Hammerstein was no Michael Moore. As for preachiness, Hammerstein was, a few years later, even preachier in *South Pacific* and was praised for it.

Since Hammerstein was a sentimentalist to the core, one might have expected him to see that his hero, Joe, and Joe's childhood sweetheart, Jenny, would marry and, after surmounting various dramatic crises, live happily ever after, like Curley and Laurie in *Oklahoma!* They do marry, but Jenny, as mentioned, is an unwholesome influence on her husband, and it is clear by the end of the play that the two will go their separate ways, she to Mr. Bigmoney, he back to his hometown – with, we surmise, his nurse Emily, played by the brilliant Miss Kirk. So, while the play had its share of saccharine, it also had an edge to it.

An aspect of *Allegro* that brought critical censure was its Greek chorus, which was placed on stage to give voice to certain emotions felt, but unsaid, by the principals. The chorus thus sang the determination of the infant Joe Taylor to walk ("One Foot, Other Foot") and the scheming thoughts of his sweetheart Jenny as she bends his will to hers. At pivotal moments the chorus is joined by ghosts from Taylor's past, including his mother and grandmother.

The chorus drew some blame for the failure of the play, but it was a clever way to present a running commentary on the action, and the lines Hammerstein gave the chorus were honest and often quite moving. As for the ghosts, they, too, were appropriate and never gimmicky. No one objected when Sondheim filled his stage with ghosts in *Follies*, nor should they have. There are times when a ghost is a handy way to bridge past and present.

Over the years, the thought of reviving *Allegro* occurred to many, including Rodgers. It is generally agreed that some rewriting is in order to reduce the preachiness quotient, but the structure of the play is sound as a dollar, and the score holds its own against 90 percent of the musicals that have opened on Broadway in the last 20 years (and against those now playing). Someday, I have no doubt, a new production of *Allegro* will open on Broadway or the West End, and playgoers will discover the gem that so delighted me back in 1947. Or maybe some enterprising community theater will take it on; it is not a difficult play to stage, once you line up the voices. A little theater in Indiana would be ideal.

After *Allegro*, Rodgers and Hammerstein created two more blockbusters, *South Pacific* and *The King and I*. Then came two flops, *Me and Juliet* and *Pipe Dream*, both long forgotten. The former deserved to fail, the latter did not.

The Rodgers & Hammerstein Flops (II)

T he failure of *Allegro* to duplicate the successes of *Oklahoma!* and *Carousel* left Rodgers and Hammerstein determined to prove that they were not two-show wonders. Their next collaboration removed any doubts along those lines.

South Pacific was a huge success, running on Broadway for 1925 performances. Richard Watts of the New York Post called it "one of the finest musical plays in the history of the American theater." Michener's tales of the South Pacific were the perfect launching pad for a string of songs that were instant classics. The show is revived often.

After *South Pacific*, they did it again in 1951, this time with *The King and I*, one of everybody's favorite R&H plays, thanks largely to the movie version starring Yul Brynner and Deborah Kerr. Today it is hard to believe that on the original playbill, Brynner's name was in small type (the star was Gertrude Lawrence) and that Brynner won his Tony that year as best *supporting* actor. If anyone ever owned a role, it was Yul Brynner as the King.

With *The King and I* packing them in at the St. James, Rodgers and Hammerstein's record was four out of five. Then, two years later, the pair opened their sixth play, *Me and Juliet*, and the record was suddenly four out of six. *Me and Juliet*, like their only previous flop, *Allegro*, was a Hammerstein creation. That is, he wrote the book as well as the lyrics. It did not escape the critics' notice that the four R&H hits had all been based on pre-existing material, while the two flops (so far) were original stories. But, while *Allegro* had much going for it (see my earlier post), *Me and Juliet* was a loser from the start.

The show is a backstage drama involving the production of a musical called *Me and Juliet*. The romantic leads are Larry, the assistant stage manager, and Jeanie, a singer in the chorus. Completing a triangle of sorts is Bob, a surly stage electrician (think of Judd Fry in *Oklahoma!*). Larry finally finds the courage to stand up to Bob, and love conquers all. Curtain.

You can't say they didn't try. Jeanie was played by the talented Isabel Bigley, who was the original Sarah Brown in *Guys and Dolls*, and Larry was played by Bill Hayes, a likeable tenor who had been a regular on Sid Caesar's television success, *Your Show of Shows*. Two other Broadway troupers were featured: Joan McCracken, one of the best dancers around at the time, and veteran character actor Ray Walston. Jo Mielziner's revolving set let the audience see the play-within-a-play from the front and the rear of the stage. The dance numbers were staged by Robert Alton, and the director was the legendary George Abbott. With all that talent, plus Rodgers and Hammerstein, how could you miss?

But in the end, ironically, it was the dynamic duo that did the show in. The book was trite and occasionally unpleasant, and the glorious Rodgers music audiences had come to expect was just not there. One song – "No Other Love" – achieved some popularity. (Rodgers used the same melody in the television documentary, *Victory at Sea*.) A ballad called "I'm Your Girl" was lovely, and I wish Rodgers had saved it for a better show. The other songs ranged from pedestrian to terrible. I remember, wincing, "The Big Black Giant" (a metaphor for an audience), the cutesy "Keep It Gay," the even cutesier "It's Me," a dreadful number called "French-Fried Potatoes and a T-Bone Steak," and, worst of all, a song called "The Theater is Dying," which was presumably intended to be satirical.

The critics groaned. Robert Coleman of the New York Daily Mirror wrote: "had it been penned by a couple of tyros named Joe Smith and Harold Jones, we would probably write this morning that it was a fair start, showing promise of sorts. But coming from the atelier of the masters it was, to put it kindly, incredible."

Despite a near-unanimous panning, the box office advance sale was strong enough to propel *Me and Juliet* through 358 performances and a small profit for its backers. The names Rodgers and Hammerstein could still sell tickets, but their reputation had just taken a body blow.

Shows about shows are tricky things. There is a starting assumption that a Broadway audience is by definition interested in show business, even the backstage goings-on. But what really grabs an audience is dramatic conflict of the type so thrillingly presented in *South Pacific, Carousel,* and *The King and I.* Shows within shows can succeed – witness Cole Porter's *Kiss Me Kate* – but there must be more for the audience to chew on than whether the stage manager or the electrician gets the girl. Above all, there must be good show tunes, which *Me and Juliet* so clearly lacked.

Me and Juliet sank without a trace. It has never been revived on Broadway, and you won't find it playing the summer theater circuit. It is best forgotten, and I bring it up only because this is, after all, a series on flops. I have the cast recording; needless to say, I don't play it often.

("Every cloud, etc." department: During the play's run, director George Abbott was on the prowl for a choreographer for his next musical, *The Pajama Game.* Cast member Joan McCracken suggested her husband, who had no credentials at all, but who nevertheless managed to win the job. His name was Bob Fosse.)

For their next show, the masters based their play on stories and characters created by the novelist John Steinbeck, and Rodgers gave the play one of his best scores. But the result was another flop.

The Rodgers & Hammerstein Flops (III)

We had been married only six months before, but Jill was already learning that life was going to be one long parade of musicals. In 1955, the musical event of the season was the new Rodgers and Hammerstein show, *Pipe Dream*. The buzz was that it would be a good one. After misfiring with *Allegro* and *Me and Juliet*, both written by Hammerstein, the masters were returning to the well that had given them their hits - the established works of established writers. The established writer in this case was John Steinbeck, whose novel *Sweet Thursday* was a sequel to *Cannery Row*, with the same colorful characters from the Monterey Peninsula.

So we made our way to the Colonial in Boston with high expectations, and we were not disappointed. The score was one of the Rodgers's best, and it was well sung by Bill Johnson, Judy Tyler, and, from the Met, Helen Traubel. In New York, where the advance sale was the largest in Broadway history, *Pipe Dream* was bound to be a smash.

In fact, it was a flop, the first and only Rodgers and Hammerstein show to lose money. What happened? Listening to the original cast album today, I still can't understand why this show failed so miserably. Well, actually, I can. When a musical with a great score fails, the fault rarely lies with the cast or the direction or the orchestrations or the scenery. The culprit almost always is the libretto. That was certainly true in this case.

The chief characters of *Pipe Dream* are a free-lance marine biologist called Doc, a girl of the street named Suzy, a good-hearted bawdy-house madam, Fauna, who gives Suzy shelter, and a gaggle of Monterey layabouts who provide the local color. Suzy introduces herself to this menagerie and to us by singing one of the most haunting songs in the R&H canon. She begins:

Scooted out of Frisco over Route 101
Bummed a ride as far as San Jose
Rode aboard a Greyhound till I run out of dough
Landed on my can in Monterey
But I saw a lot of things along the way.
And I did a lot of thinking on the way.

Suzy then slips into the chorus of the plaintive "Everybody's Got a Home But Me."

I rode by a house with the window lighted up
Looking brighter than a Christmas tree
And I said to myself, as I rode by myself
Everybody's got a home but me.

The melody is one of Rodgers's best, and it is worth noting that while the composer was writing and rewriting the superb melodies of *Pipe Dream* he was diagnosed with cancer and underwent emergency surgery to remove part of his jaw. When he left the hospital, he immediately resumed work on the show – with gusto. The man loved his work.

The source material, *Sweet Thursday*, was fairly spicy stuff, especially for Hammerstein, who set about "cleaning it up." Steinbeck's Suzy is unequivocally a prostitute, but, complained the novelist later, Hammerstein turned her into a visiting nurse. The madam, played by diva Traubel, sings about "The Happiest House on the Block" as innocently and joyously as if she were leading a gospel sing.

Conventional wisdom says that from the outset the material was wrong for Hammerstein, and this may well be true (in retrospect, Rodgers thought so), but like *Allegro*, *Pipe Dream* could be rewritten into the smash hit it promised to be. Take the moralizing out of *Allegro*, put the earthiness back into *Pipe Dream*, and you have two potential hits.

Bill Johnson was plucked from the cast of *Kismet* for the part of Doc. Johnson was a veteran leading man, with a rich, pleasing baritone voice, best displayed here in "The Man I Used To Be." Judy Tyler, who played Suzy, was a newcomer to Broadway, and her good looks and strong, deep voice seemed to promise a successful career on Broadway. Tragically, both Tyler and Johnson were dead less than a year after *Pipe Dream* opened, he of a heart attack at 40, she in a car crash at 23.

Pipe Dream was the third and last of the R&H flops. Their next show, *Flower Drum Song*, was a hit, running more than 600 performances, and their last show was the epic *The Sound of Music*, which notched 1433 performances. Final accounting: nine shows, eight money-makers, six solid hits. The full record should include the popular movie musical *State Fair* and the hugely successful TV production of *Cinderella*, both of which featured excellent scores.

Both Rodgers and Hammerstein were giants of the theater even before they began to collaborate – Rodgers with Larry Hart, Hammerstein with, among others, Jerome Kern. (The memorable lyrics for *Show Boat* were Hammerstein's.) But when these two creative geniuses decided to work together, the result was a "perfect storm" of theater magic. Broadway will never see their like again.

Broadway Memories

Since I had the good fortune to spend most of my life in the Boston area and to travel regularly to New York City, I was able to see most of the "Golden Era" musicals in their Boston tryouts or opening runs or performed by national touring companies. I saw some of the Rodgers and Hammerstein classics and even their missteps (*Pipe Dream, Allegro*). I was able to see Jerry Orbach, Gwen Verdon, Phil Silvers, Richard Kiley, John Raitt, Chita Rivera, and many other Broadway titans at the peaks of their careers. I saw Tommy Tune in his first Broadway musical, *SeeSaw*. I was knocked out by Diahann Carroll in *No Strings*. I bought standing room to see the original *The Most Happy Fella*. Boy, those were the days, and those were the plays.

Theater memories abound. One Saturday evening in 1961, Jill and I saw *Camelot* in New York. It turned out that a friend was in the cast, and we parlayed this fact into an invitation to join him backstage after the final curtain. The show was well into its run at the time, so the usual backstage claques had thinned out. Our friend led us into Richard Burton's dressing room, where we spent a memorable half hour with Burton, Julie Andrews, Robert Goulet, and Roddy McDowall. Burton was charming, deflecting any comments about his work by insisting on knowing more about us and our lives. It is easy to see why so many women were in thrall. The others were just as pleasant and chatty.

That afternoon we had attended a matinee of another musical, *Donnybrook!,* based on the film *The Quiet Man*. It was a passable show, with a few too many "begorrahs" for its own good. As it happened, on that very day it was announced that *Donnybrook!* would soon close after only 68 performances. This news was filtering throughout the backstage area at the Majestic while we were shmoozing with the *Camelot* cast, and it was clear that the news was a downer to the entire company. It may have been another show, in another theater, but it was a death in the family.

In 1958 the musical *Goldilocks* opened its pre-Broadway run at Boston's Shubert Theater. The show had a brilliant score, with music by Leroy Anderson and clever lyrics by Walter and Jean Kerr. As happens often, a first-rate score was sabotaged by an inferior book, and in New York it managed only a 20-week run. (The original-cast recording is highly recommended.) What I remember most about that show was an après theater drinking session with Rudy Vallee (friend of a friend) at a hotel bar. In Boston, the *Goldilocks* male lead was being played by Barry Sullivan, a decent movie actor but obviously out of place in a musical. Vallee, suspecting that the producers would insist on a replacement, was hovering at the ready. We chatted for about three quarters of an hour.

There was some common ground: Jean Kerr had written a comedy, *Jenny Kissed Me*, some years earlier, and Vallee and I had both acted in that play, he in stock, I in college. I had fond memories of the experience but was not allowed to share them, for Vallee, unlike Richard Burton, had a monumental ego and monopolized the conversation. In this I was only too happy to indulge him, as his stories were good, and besides, if a professional entertainer can't flex his ego, who can? Anyway, his instincts about the *Goldilocks* leading man were on the money, but in the event the part went to Don Ameche, who carried it off quite well on Broadway.

Three years later, Vallee would get his chance in a musical, nailing the good role of J.J. Biggley in *How to Succeed in Business Without Really Trying*. In the 1960s, if you were in New York for a weekend, your problem was not finding a good show but in choosing which hit to see. Would it be *Fiddler on the Roof*? *Hello Dolly*? *West Side Story*? *The Music Man*? They were all on offer within a few blocks. The only challenge was to get tickets. Today, if you are in the market for a new Broadway musical, your choices are *Rent, Hairspray*, and *Avenue Q*. There is also *A Light in the Piazza*, by Adam Guettel, who, as Richard Rodgers's grandson, might be expected to have inherited a few melody genes. But I detected none.

Many others have lamented the end of the Golden Era of musicals, hastened by the Beatles and rock and roll, and I have nothing to add except to point out that all that glorious music, sung by those legendary Broadway performers, still exists, courtesy of CDs, tapes, and LP records. And it is a real treat to discover one of those choice scores that fell victim to a bad book and consequently drifted into obscurity. I have quite a few such treasures, some of which are described in this book.

Who Lost Those Treasures, Anyway?

Hollywood often makes a hash of it when it takes a good Broadway musical and turns it into a motion picture. Examples of hash abound: *Gypsy*, *Mame,* and *Hello Dolly!* top the list. Replacing Ethel Merman with Rosalind Russell was downright criminal, as was replacing Lansbury with Ball and Channing with Streisand. So we are left without the definitive records of these shows, the Broadway versions. Bummer. Maybe the technology wasn't available then, but it is now, and there is no excuse for not creating a DVD of every good musical that makes it to the Great White Way.

Money shouldn't be a problem. Just as film producers make more money today from DVD sales than from the box-office, the DVDs of musicals, even the mediocre ones, should be able to recover their costs and then some. I recently watched the DVD of *Barnum*, filmed at a live performance in London. Okay, it was Michael Crawford and not Jim Dale, but no complaint there. I have on tape a BBC presentation of *She Loves Me* and while it's better then nothing, how I would like to have the original Broadway cast, with Barbara Cook. There have been pretty good PBS productions of *Cats, Into the Woods, Sweeney Todd, A Light in the Piazza*, and *Sundays in the Park with Geor*ge. But for every musical that is available on DVD, there are at least 100 that are not. What I would give for a DVD of the original *Most Happy Fella*, with Robert Weede or *No Strings* with

Richard Kiley and Diahann Carroll or *Follies* with Dorothy Collins and Gene Nelson and Alexis Smith. Why did no one preserve those original-cast performances, the way they preserved original cast recordings? More to the point, why aren't they preserving them today? Scraps of film survive, and some of these have been assembled into two DVDs called "Lost Treasures." The first of these is by far the better, featuring John Raitt, Julie Andrews, Joel Grey, Robert Preston, Jerry Orbach, and others singing their signature songs. It's good to have them, but it also raises a question: Who lost the treasures in the first place?

If a show is a real blockbuster, Hollywood will get around to it. And, to be fair, sometimes the film-makers do a good job. *Evita* was a good film, and *Oliver!* (from the UK, not Hollywood) was flat-out brilliant. We can still see Merman in *Call Me Madam*, Gwen Verdon in *Damn Yankees*, John Raitt in *The Pajama Game*, and Robert Preston in *The Music Man*. More recently, *The Producers* was filmed with its original Broadway stars, Nathan Hale and Matthew Broderick.

But the vast majority of Broadway musicals disappear without a trace. We will never see Sid Caesar in *Little Me* or Phil Silvers in *Do Re Mi* or Robert Lindsay in *Me and My Girl*, all *tour de force* performances. Die-hard Broadway aficionados trade in bootleg copies of videotapes made by various members of the cast or crew, or by people who sneak videocams into the theater. They are typically herky-jerky, with atrocious audio quality, but some people will put up with this to snatch a glimpse of the real thing. If a decent real thing existed, the bootleggers would be out of business. It's a shame. Musical theater is the one art form at which this country surpasses all others. Artistic history has been made on Broadway, but no one bothered to capture it for posterity. This sin of omission continues today, and that's a mystery to me, because the producers are leaving real money on the table.

Sondheim

Stephen Sondheim was a protégé of Oscar Hammerstein II. In fact, Sondheim calls Hammerstein a surrogate father. A comparison of the two master lyricists is fascinating. In their outlooks on life as expressed by their lyrics, they were exact opposites. Hammerstein was a romantic poet, drawn to the celebration of life's simple pleasures. In Hammerstein's world, people fall in love, singing "Don't sigh and gaze at me; your sighs are so like mine. Your eyes mustn't glow like mine; people will say we're in love" - all against a backdrop of June bustin' out all over or a bright golden haze on the meadow.

Sondheim wouldn't be caught dead wallowing in such sentimentality. In his universe, married couples suffer "every day a little death" and wives assault their husbands for "passionless love-making once a year" and "the lies ill-concealed and the wounds never healed." Sondheim is a cynic, if not a nihilist, and his focus is on the frustrations of life ("the road I didn't take") and the capacity of man to inflict and to suffer pain.

Hammerstein was by far the greater commercial success, and nothing Sondheim has ever written approaches the popularity of *Oklahoma!* or *Carousel*. Still, it would be a mistake to write Sondheim off as a misanthropic failure. For openers, remember that Sondheim the brilliant lyricist is also Sondheim the talented composer. He does not have the ability to craft an endless succession of melodic tunes, as did Hammerstein's partner, Richard Rodgers, but his music is inventive, with a tart flavor well suited to the lyrics. ("Too Many Mornings," from *Follies*, is a sterling example.) Will Sondheim's creations still be around 100 years from now? Absolutely – as will the creations of Rodgers and Hammerstein. The glass is both half full and half empty.

These thoughts flitted through my mind last night as I watched a DVD called *Putting it Together*, a compilation of Sondheim's theater songs. This is a 1999 Cameron Mackintosh production, so you know it must be first-rate. And boy, is it ever! The performers are show biz veterans George Hearn and Carol Burnett, along with three young British actors: John Barrowman, Ruthie Henshall, and Bronson Pinchot. The singing, the choreography, the orchestrations (Jonathan Tunick, of course), and the technical quality of the DVD leave little to be desired. Barrowman and Henshall were both born for the musical stage, Carol Burnett seems to get better with age, and George Hearn, still strong-voiced, is worth studying as an exercise in vocal acting. One or two of Sondheim's more acidic songs may turn you off, but most of the material is choice, and the talent is stunning. If you like musical theater, grab this one. You won't find a more stylish, more polished execution of the Sondheim repertoire anywhere.

Operetta Lives!

Andrew Lloyd Webber often cites Richard Rodgers as the popular composer he most admires. Rodgers, in turn, often acknowledged his debt to Jerome Kern, who is generally credited for inventing American theater music as we now know it, especially with his 1927 score for *Showboat*. But who was Kern's role model? It was Victor Herbert, whose name is often preceded by "The Great" or "The Immortal." Herbert was the master of theater music in the early twentieth century. His *Naughty Marietta, The Red Mill, Eileen, The Fortune Teller*, and *Babes in Toyland* were the blockbusters of their day, destined to be revived again and again on Broadway. Herbert was no tin-pan-alley noodler. Born in Dublin of German parents, he studied at the Stuttgart Conservatory, was a cellist for the Met, and conductor of the Pittsburgh Symphony. He was, in short, a serious, talented musician and maestro. But his place in history is defined by his achievements as a composer.

Herbert's field was operetta. Operetta was a very big deal on Broadway a century ago, thanks to Herbert, as well as Sigmund Romberg (*The Desert Song, The Student Prince, Maytime, Blossom Time*), Franz Lehar (*The Merry Widow*), and many other composers, mostly European. Emmerich Kalman, almost forgotten today, was one of the best, and "Stars of the Stage," from his *The Bayadere*, is one of the most beautiful theater songs you'll never hear.

The plots were silly, usually set in exotic lands and dealing with princes, rights of succession, pirates, buffoons, and assorted strange characters, all colorfully costumed, and all overacting. In the U.S., operettas were sung in English (in translation), which made them much more accessible to the masses than grand opera. The audiences loved them, for one reason: the music. And what music it was!

But alas, operetta is now long gone from the scene, and if you want to watch a full-bore, no-compromise production of, say, *The New Moon*, you are out of luck. You were born 60 or 70 years too late.

Or maybe not. There is still a place where you can see operetta as it should be performed, which means with the great voices, full orchestra, and professionally executed costumes and scenery that these productions demand. I am talking about the Ohio Light Opera Company.

The OLO holds forth each summer at the Freedlander Theater on the campus of Wooster College, in Wooster Ohio, where it began as a Gilbert and Sullivan troupe about 25 years ago. Today its repertoire is mostly the kind of operettas I've been talking about, plus one classic Broadway musical and at least one Gilbert and Sullivan. The plays are rotated throughout the season, so that it is possible to cover four or five plays during a week's visit. This is exactly what Jill and I have done twice in recent years, driving to Wooster, putting up in a local hotel, driving to the Freedlander each evening and letting the OLO time machine carry us back to the days when operetta was king.

Wooster is in the northeast part of Ohio, in Amish country, where the restaurants serve hearty home-cooked meals. You won't find a Hyatt Regency in Wooster, but the accommodations in the area are more than adequate.

After each season, the OLO issues CDs of a couple of the plays, and at this point there is a fairly extensive catalog of operettas, if you would like to sample the quality. These CDs contain the entire plays, not just the music. (Personally, I would rather have just the songs.)

This summer's program includes *The New Moon* (Romberg), *The Firefly* (Friml), *The Queen's Lace Handkerchief* (Strauss), *HMS Pinafore, The Gondoliers,* and *Pride and Prejudice*. The season runs from mid-June to mid-August. You can find out more at www.wooster.edu/ohiolightopera.

I must in conscience add that the Wooster area, despite the blandishments of the local tourist office, is not exactly teeming with sightseeing attractions (lots of corn fields), so you may find the days, um, uneventful. We solved this problem by scheduling a couple of OLO matinees during our stay. If you like good music, this is not a bad way to spend a week, especially if you have friends or other business in Ohio.

Along the Rialto in Maine

Stratford-on-Saco

The theater season is in full swing here in Maine, I am glad to report. It is now possible to see a different play each week without traveling more than an hour from home. Good theater seems to be plentiful in the State, even in some unlikely places.

Like Bar Mills. This little dot on the map lies on the banks of the Saco River, about 25 miles west of here. In fact, the theater itself, the 109-year-old Grange Hall, sits precariously on the banks of this river, which is quite busy at this point in its flow from New Hampshire to the Atlantic.

The other night Jill and I drove to Bar Mills to see *Communicating Doors*, by the acclaimed British playwright Alan Ayckbourn (*Relatively Speaking*, *Season's Greetings*). Mr. Ayckbourn's plots tend to be devilishly clever, and his characters are not the kind of people you generally find in Maine. So the first surprise was that the Bar Mills theater group, which calls itself "The Originals," would choose the play. The second surprise was that the cast of six was so good and so well directed. The third surprise was that the sell-out audience lapped it up so enthusiastically. But I shouldn't have been surprised by any of this; it is always a mistake to underestimate the intelligence and taste of small-town America.

The plot of *Communicating Doors* defies explanation, but let's try. A prostitute who calls herself Poopay arrives in a hotel suite at the invitation of a septuagenarian named Reece, who has engaged her, not for her professional services, but to witness a confession involving the long-ago murders of his two wives. The other characters are Reece's stone-faced business partner Julian, Reece's wives 1 and 2, and a security guard at the hotel where all the action takes place.

Julian, deeply implicated in the murders, becomes a mortal threat to Poopay once she has read Reece's confession. In the course of fleeing Julian, Poopay finds that one of the doors in the suite sends her back in time, where she meets each of Reese's wives and tries to warn her about what lies in store. Poopay can use this door to travel from the present (2014) to the past (1994, wife 2) to the more distant past (1974, wife 1) and back again, but each wife can travel only backward, never forward beyond her own time. If this sounds confusing, it is, but the cast played it all intelligently and seriously, nailing the funny bits (which were abundant) without cracking a smile. The time-warp plot has a certain mathematical integrity, but that's beside the point. The characters are interesting, the dialog sparkles, and there is enough tension to keep the audience on edge. Ayckbourn called his play a "comedy/thriller," and it is exactly that.

The single set was a work of art and the costumes just right (Poopay makes her entrance in a skin-tight black net affair that sets the tone for the evening), but it was the actors' reverence for the material that made the evening so special. All six were skilled actors, but the Tony goes to Jennifer Porter, a perfect Poopay who avoided the stock poses of the hooker in favor of a simple, honest portrayal of a girl who just wants to be good at her specialty. (She is, she says, a dominatrix, and she has the whip to prove it.) Ms Porter also gave Poopay a most credible cockney accent.

A ticket at the Bar Mills Grange Hall can be had for as little as $10. There's only one catch: Tickets sell out quickly. The folks around Bar Mills are no fools.

The Final Cut

Biddeford's Jewel

But there are fools aplenty in Neil Simon's *Fools*, which was staged recently at the Biddeford City Theater. We saw it on opening night, and it was a treat, as most Simon plays are if they are competently presented, as this one was. *Fools* takes place, not in Simon's usual New York beat, but a century ago in a Ukrainian village called Kulyenchikov. A young schoolteacher, Leon, arrives in the village in the play's opening scene, eager to tackle his first assignment. He soon discovers that all the residents of Kulyenchikov are stupid, owing to a 200-year-old curse. The dumb-as-dirt villagers we meet include the mailman, the baker, the doctor and his wife and their beautiful daughter Sophia, who steals Leon's heart. They are all reasonably articulate people, just smart enough to know that they are stupid, and why. The combination of a bright young schoolteacher and a flock of stupid villagers is a perfect setup for the kind of zingy one-liners no one writes better than Neil Simon.

The play was good, but to me the real star of the evening was the theater itself, the City Theater (or Salle d'Opera) in Biddeford, Maine. The theater is 110 years old, and in its heyday it was an important stop on the New England vaudeville circuit. Biddeford was a thriving city then, with enormous textile mills employing thousands of mostly French-Canadian workers, and the Salle d'Opera was packed when the headliners came to town. And what headliners! Fred Astaire danced on the stage, W.C.

147

Fields told jokes, Laurel and Hardy clowned, and Mae West did, well, whatever Mae West did.

When vaudeville faded, the Opera House became a movie house. Then it closed, and it seemed only a matter of time before it was hauled down. What saved it, probably, was its location adjoining the City Hall. It was handy storage space for the municipality, serving, at its low point, as a repository for the City's gravel.

I won't keep you in suspense. Today it has been lovingly restored. The proscenium is classic. New seats fill the orchestra and the large balcony, with its gracefully curved façade. The walls have been repainted, the floors refinished. The entrance and staircase to the second-floor lobby feature dark, paneled hardwood, red carpeting, and a welcoming, old-world ambiance.

Across the country, there are probably hundreds of old theaters, empty and abandoned, awaiting the wrecking ball. Once they're gone, they're gone forever. We shouldn't let it happen.

As for Leon the schoolteacher, he breaks the curse, liberates the village, and marries Sophia, who is now as smart as she is beautiful. Neil Simon wouldn't let you down.

The World Goes 'Round

Having been impressed by a production of Ayckbourn's *Communicating Doors* at the Grange Hall in Bar Mills (see my post "Along the Rialto"), I nevertheless approached *The World Goes 'Round* by the same theater group with some trepidation. The handful of performers that form the backbone of "The Originals" were excellent actors, but it's a long way from British farce to a musical based on the songs of Kander and Ebb. I needn't have worried; "The Originals" are musically as well as dramatically talented, and the show was a solid success.

John Kander and Fred Ebb were a bit of an odd couple. Kander, from the Midwest, was a classically trained musician whose passion was opera. He was soft-spoken and laid back. Ebb, from New York, was mercurial and the life of the party. Kander was a masterful theater composer, able to adapt his style to any style or period (think of "Wilkommen" from *Cabaret*), and Ebb was a brilliant writer who often wove topical humor into his lyrics. They are the perfect pair to showcase in a review, because their songs don't require setups. Although many of the songs in the review are situational, you don't need to know anything about the story line for "Arthur in the Afternoon" to get its humor. In fact, I can't think of a single one of the 25 or so songs chosen for the show that needed any explanation at all.

Most of the songs were from Broadway musicals (*Chicago*, *Cabaret*, *The Act*, *The Rink*, etc.), but there were also what Fred Ebb liked to call "party songs" like "Sara Lee" and "special material" written for a specific performer or TV special, like "Liza with a Z."

The songs were performed by a cast of five: two local couples (Jennifer Porter and Dana Packard, the theater's directors, and Jim and Molly Roberts) and one ringer, the attractive and outrageously talented Susan Brownfield, whose Broadway experience was obvious the moment she walked onstage. Ms. Brownfield was the star of the evening, whose offering of "Colored Lights" was memorable, but the other four performers all had their moments, too.

Molly, like the other ladies stunning in a black dress, launched the evening with the title song and was terrific in "Ring Them Bells." Dana Packard was hilarious rhapsodizing about Sara Lee's cherry Danish, Jim Roberts gave "The Kiss of the Spider Woman" the dramatic intensity that song demands, and the multi-talented Jennifer Porter sang the wistful ballad "It's a Quiet Thing" (Kander's own favorite) and waltzed with husband Dana to "Heiraten."

Several ensemble numbers were show-stoppers, notably "Me and My Baby," in which all five played banjos, the frantic "Coffee in a Cardboard Cup," "The Rink," in which the cast risked life and limb on roller skates, and

"Cabaret," in a close-harmony, jazzy arrangement that ended the show.

Special mention must be made of the three musicians who accompanied the performers from behind a scrim: David Libby on piano, Jim Lyden on bass, and Les Harris, Jr. on drums. They are all professional-grade artists, and they provided exactly the right musical settings, especially for "Maybe This Time," which is essentially a duet for vocalist and piano. John Kander would have been pleased.

Kander and Ebb were masters of the musical theater art. Fred Ebb died last year, so their book is closed. But the music, as they say, lives on. Many people in the audience probably never heard of Kander and Ebb before they came to the Bar Mills Grange Hall, and now they have. There's a certain satisfaction to be gained from that. Music like this and its creators deserve to be remembered.

I Love a Piano

The other night we attended a performance of *I Love a Piano* at the Arundel Barn Playhouse, just down the road a few miles. ILAP is a compilation of popular songs written by Irving Berlin. Dick Rodgers, Cole Porter, Jerome Kern, Harry Warren, and George Gershwin were all great composers, but Berlin was in a class by himself. He wrote waltzes, love ballads, comedy songs, anthems, holiday songs, and he was a master of each form. It is impossible to characterize a "Berlin song," because there's no such thing. 'God Bless America" has nothing in common with "White Christmas," which has nothing in common with "I Got Lost in His Arms."

I can understand how someone can become a brain surgeon or an architect; there are established procedures one can learn and practice. But I will never understand how Irving Berlin can create something like "Say it Isn't So" or "Suppertime." Not just the fabulous melodies, but the lyrics, in which the right syllable always falls on the right note. There's no rational explanation; you just shrug your shoulders and say "genius."

The people who put together *I Love a Piano* chose sixty Berlin songs to mount. Most were familiar, but a few were rarely heard numbers, like "Pack Up Your Sins and Take Them to the Devil." Each was set up with a story line, each required a fair amount of business and choreography and costuming. Six performers – three men, three women – sang their way through all the material, all of which was created before they were born, and, shortcomings aside, it was reassuring to see the younger generation showing such respect for the work of the master.

The six performers were all talented, but not extravagantly so. Christopher Lengerich, a tall, thin

Jimmy Stewart type, was the best of the lot. He could dance, and he sang passably. An elfin female dancer (Katherine Mills) was cute and sang well, but she lacked spark (friends who accompanied us suggested that she was ailing). Bridie Carroll, looking like an oversized Alice Faye, handled "Suppertime" well, and the most spirited performer of all, James Ryan Sloan, did a terrific job on "Oh, How I Hate to Get Up in the Morning." But all in all, the best that can be said of the cast is that they worked hard, had the lyrics down pat, and sang them so that you could understand every word.

A show like this obviously requires a topnotch pianist, and this show had one of the best in Paul Feyer. I wish he had a better instrument to work with, but others thought a tired old piano was more in keeping with the theme (a beat-up old upright, through the years).

On the stage, there is a gulf of some magnitude between a very good amateur and a professional. Once in a while – very rarely – amateurs can bridge that gulf. But this troupe did not.

Nevertheless, the evening was very enjoyable. The Berlin repertoire will always carry the day unless the performers are awful, and this cast was definitely not that. So I can recommend the show. After all, how often do you get to hear sixty Irving Berlin songs at one sitting?

Irving Berlin wrote 899 copyrighted songs. How an immigrant child, speaking no English when he came to America, became the greatest songwriter in history is a fascinating story. The definitive biography is Laurence Bergreen's "As Thousands Cheer." If you like popular music, it's a must.

– – – – – – – – – – – – – –

Giuditta

A beautiful but bored housewife in a Mediterranean port city (let's say Barcelona) charms an Army captain who is en route to a campaign in a North African city (let's say Tangiers) and impulsively takes off with him, and the two live together in his villa in North Africa. But duty calls, and he must leave her to join his regiment. She begs him to stay, but he marches off, more than a little worried that the men of North Africa may be drawn to her like ants to a picnic.

His worries are well founded, for after a while she is an exotic dancer in a nightclub, where her charms are irresistible to the club's well heeled patrons. The captain finally deserts his regiment and tracks her down, but it is too late: She has found a life that agrees with her.

Years later, the broken-hearted captain is reduced to working as a cocktail pianist in a luxury hotel. His old flame is ushered to a table to await her escort for the evening, a wealthy duke. The captain plays a few bars of "their" old song (no, it's not "As Time Goes By'), and she recognizes him and tries to restart the old romance. Alas, this time it's too late for him, for he's a broken man. The girl leaves with the duke.

That is the plot of Franz Lehar's last major operetta, *Giuditta*, which premiered in Vienna in 1934, about 30 years after Lehar wrote what is probably the most successful operetta of all time, *The Merry Widow*. The Vienna premiere of "Giuditta" (Lehar's favorite) was broadcast worldwide by no fewer than 120 radio stations, but for all that, it was not well received by the locals, and to this day it has never been seen in New York, London, or Paris.

Has your curiosity been piqued? Good, because I am here to tell you that a fine CD recording exists, in English, courtesy of Telarc. It stars Jerry Hadley, familiar to all PBS fans, as Octavio, the captain, and Deborah Riedel in the title role. A full-bodied English Chamber Orchestra backs them up, and the excellent program booklet includes the entire libretto. You may recognize a couple of the songs: "Love, Gentle and Tender" and "Kiss My Lips and Your Heart's Aflame" (both woeful translations of the original German). The CD was recorded in London in 1996, and it is technically very good. Hadley, a superb tenor, is in good voice. Riedel is a capable soprano, if a bit shrill at times. The secondary couple (there's always a secondary couple in these things) are Naomi Itami and Lynton Atkinson, both solid performers.

Follies

Few musicals have inspired the kind of passionate debate that surrounds *Follies*. With music and lyrics by Stephen Sondheim, direction by Hal Prince, choreography by Michael Bennett, and book by James Goldman, here is a show created by Broadway's A-Team of the era. It tells a simple story: Old-time Follies girls and their husbands get together for a reunion party at the old theater, about to be torn down. But nothing from Sondheim is ever simple. The Follies girls of old have since experienced the follies of life. The principals – two women and their husbands – are forced to relive the fun times of yesteryear (their young alter egos are actually on stage with them) and see how terribly wrong it all turned out in the years since. In other words, the girls, Sally and Phyllis, and their husbands, Buddy and Ben, have all wound up deep in the heart of Sondheimland, sadder but wiser (but sadder).

In the years since, critics have split on the merits of the show. For some, this is Sondheim's masterpiece, with supremely clever lyrics like:

Say, Mister producer,
I'm talking to you, sir
I don't need a lot
Only what I've got
Plus a tube of greasepaint
And a follow spot.

as well as emotionally rich melodies, such as those of "Losing My Mind" and "Too Many Mornings."

Others, including the *New York Times* drama critic, found the subject matter off-putting. The show was a financial failure, partly because it was so expensive to mount, and revivals (rare, because of the cost) have similarly lost money. Several cast and concert recordings are available on CD, each with its own fans and its own detractors.

After the original New York production closed, the company moved to the Shubert Theater in Los Angeles, and it was there I saw the original Sally (Dorothy Collins), Phyllis (Alexis Smith), Buddy (Gene Nelson) and Ben (John McMartin). The show blew me away, and I have always counted it a creation of pure genius. I also saw the show at the Maine State Music Theater a couple of years ago. It was a first-rate production, and it confirmed my initial judgment of the show's quality.

Then, this year, my daughter gave me a copy of a new book called *Everything Was Possible*, by Ted Chapin. The author, a college student in 1971, managed to land a job as a gofer for *Follies* through its gestation in New York, its trial run at Boston's Colonial Theater, and its Broadway opening. The book is superb on at least two levels: For anyone who likes a good, suspenseful story with fascinating characters, here are over-the-hill performers (like Carlotta, played by Yvonne De Carlo), yearning for one more star turn, the outsized egos of

Prince, Sondheim, Bennett, etc, each trying to twist *Follies* into his own vision. (Fortunately, and amazingly, the visions were not that far apart.)

On another level the book is essentially a master's thesis on the creation of a professional Broadway musical. Most of us think of a musical as a happy marriage of book, music, lyrics, and choreography. But that's just to get the ball rolling. There are literally hundreds of other details that must be attended to. How many instruments can the orchestrator count on? (For *Follies*, 28.) What materials can be used for the costumes? (For Follies girls, sequins, beads, and feathers, lots of feathers) How will daily script changes be communicated to the cast? (No word processors or CopyIt shops in 1971.) After reading Chapin's book, I must conclude that it is a miracle that any musical ever makes it to Broadway.

For Ted Chapin, 35 years later, the young dreams of a career in musical theater have been grandly realized. He is now the President of the Rodgers & Hammerstein Organization. The gofer in Sondheim's bittersweet *Follies* now sits atop the empire that controls *Oklahoma, South Pacific, Carousel, The Sound of Music*, and the rest of the R&H canon. Like the principals in *Follies*, he has revisited his past, in his case by writing a book. Unlike those unhappy folks, he ended up, not in Sondheimland, but in the land of Happy Talk.

The Summer Circuit

S ummer in New England brings with it summer theater and the chance to see the classic old musicals and to understand why they are called classics. It is also a time to catch some little gems that never made it to the provinces. In recent weeks both opportunities were available, and we seized them.

First, the classic: A full-bore, thoroughly professional *The King and I* was staged by the Reagle Players, in Waltham, MA. If you live within driving distance of Waltham (we do, barely) and have never attended a Reagle production, shame on you. In New York or Boston, you will pay three or four times the Reagle ticket price, but you will not see higher quality. For big musicals like *The King and I*, this company usually trucks in the Broadway sets and costumes, and the leads are often played by Broadway veterans. In an era when Broadway pit orchestras have been pared down to 14 or 15 musicians, there were 21 on hand for *The King and I*, and they handled the original orchestrations smoothly.

Anna was played by the incandescent Sarah Pfisterer, no stranger to Reagle and always a joy to watch. "The House of Uncle Thomas" ballet was a highlight and alone worth the price of admission. The huge cast included a large number of young, smiling, non-Caucasian children, all of them irresistible. The only sour note was the fact that there were many empty seats in the large theater the night we attended. This was unusual. In our previous Reagle excursions (*She Loves Me, Most Happy Fella, 42d Street*, etc), the house was always full, deservedly. What's the good in living in a cultural mecca like Greater Boston if you don't take advantage of treasures like The Reagle Players?

The King and I is an ambitious, expensive undertaking, beyond the capabilities of most summer theaters. But one doesn't need Rodgers and Hammerstein to provide first-rate musical entertainment. Take the group at Bar Mills, Maine, for instance. We have reported previously on this small troupe, which calls itself The Originals. Although it occasionally ventures into the mainstream repertoire, the fare is usually off-beat. This time it was off-beat and off-Broadway, as it staged the 2001 musical *The IT Girl*, based loosely on an old Paramount movie. The campy plot involves a department-store (Waltham's) sales girl (Betty Lou Spence) who aspires to win the store's IT Girl title – and, by the way, the store's owner, Jonathan Waltham. A cast of seven doubled and tripled to play 15 roles, covering both ends of the social spectrum – Waltham's upper-crust friends and Betty Lou's buddies from the tenements. The staging was creative - a clothes line for the tenements, a ship's railing for a boat picnic, and, most important, rear projections of old New York, borrowed, one guesses, from the New York production.

Susan Brownfield, the lead, was outstanding, which was no surprise to anyone who saw her in *The World Goes Round* a year ago. A Chita Rivera type, she can act, sing, and dance, and she looks terrific, too. Molly Roberts, an Originals regular, shone as the haughty fiancée who stands in the way of our heroine. The big surprise was the music, by Paul McKibbins. Especially memorable was a lullaby, "Mama's Arms," sung by Jennifer Porter, who also directed and choreographed the production. The score, which had touches of ragtime as well as Gilbert & Sullivan, was well handled by a trio of musicians, with pianist Joe Arsenault a standout.

The Reagle Players do their work in the spacious auditorium of Waltham High School. The stage is enormous, and the lighting and acoustics are first-class. The upholstered seats are reserved. The ambiance is comfortable and the curtain times sensible.

The Originals stage their productions in the cozy, quaint, century-old Saco River Grange Hall, in Bar Mills, Maine. The folding wooden chairs are not reserved, and the rest rooms are portable units outside the hall. The stage is adequate, no more. There are home-brew footlights and a spot, and some cast members were miked, though in the small theater this may not have been necessary. On the whole, the old Grange Hall represents a formidable challenge to this highly talented theatrical group, and their determined professionalism is all the more praiseworthy. Bar Mills is an easy drive for most people who live in Maine's York County. It is well worth the trip, because the product is so entertaining.

A Sense of Place

Most of us have no trouble identifying the composers and lyricists of the great musicals. Some of us can even name the choreographers, and a few can even tell you who orchestrated the score. A musical is a giant collaboration, and an army of creative people share the credit.

But here's an often-overlooked ingredient, one that often makes the difference: the setting.

Think of the Kander-Ebb classic *Chicago* set in, say, Detroit. It doesn't work. The score, lyrics, and book all feed off Chicago's raucous reputation. Or think of *My Fair Lady* set anywhere except London. How about *On The Town* set in Boston instead of New York? Impossible.

The favorite settings for musicals are New York (*42d Street, West Side Story, Chorus Line, Annie, Fiorello!* etc), Paris (*Irma La Douce, No Strings, Silk Stockings, Phantom of the Opera*), London (*Oliver!, My Fair Lady, Me and My Girl, Baker Street*), and Los Angeles (*City of Angels, Mack & Mabel, Sunset Boulevard*). But other cities have contributed their own unique personalities. *Fanny* was perfectly set in Marseilles, a salty city where a young man could easily fall prey to the siren call of the sea. (Marseilles's harbor is glorious in the film, one of

162

my favorites.) San Francisco was just the right setting for *Flower Drum Song*, and Budapest was equally perfect for *She Loves Me*. Hollywood vacillated, setting that story first in Budapest (*Shop Around the Corner*), then in Chicago (*In The Good Old Summertime*). Rodgers and Hammerstein turned Molnar's *Liliom* into *Carousel*, in the process transplanting the story from Hungary to the coast of Maine. (What do people have against Hungary, anyway?)

History mandated that *Evita* be in Buenos Aires, *1776* in Philadelphia, and *Miss Saigon* in Vietnam. *South Pacific* and *The Sound of Music* are also historically rooted in specific locales. Romantic musicals with lots of waltzes are just right for Venice (*Do I Hear a Waltz?*) or Vienna (*The Gay Life*). If you need a dull place where your hero is so bored that he would give his soul to escape, try Washington, DC (*Damn Yankees*).

Sometimes the ideal city for a given musical doesn't exist and must be invented. Thus we have Camelot, Anatevka, River City, and Brigadoon, none of which appears in my *Times Atlas of the World,* although it is possible that once every hundred years the editors will give in and show us where in the Scottish highlands we will find Brigadoon.

.

I Remember Mama

My association with *I Remember Mama* began in 1948, when I played Papa in a college production of the John Van Druten play. In the following years I was among millions who enjoyed the movie with Irene Dunne and the immensely popular TV series with Peggy Wood. The movie seems dated today, which is strange because the play itself is a flashback, whose charm lies very much in its datedness.

I Remember Mama is a gentle story about a Norwegian family in 1910 San Francisco. Mama is the all-knowing, all-understanding, caring woman who embodies the best qualities we all associate with our mothers. Papa is hard-working, dutiful, and, as far as his contribution to the story goes, wallpaper. This is Mama's story, as told by one of her daughters, Katrin. The other characters are Katrin's sisters, her brother Nels, some busybody aunts, and Uncle Chris, a rich curmudgeon. They all exist in the play only to create opportunities for Mama to prove what a magnificent presence she is.

The story originated in a book by Kathryn Forbes called *Mama's Bank Account.* The bank account is a fiction perpetrated by Mama to give her children a sense of security. There is no bank account, but the family has something far more valuable: a mother who is infinitely wise and resourceful.

The Van Druten play, starring Mady Christian as Mama, was a smash hit, running 713 performances from 1944 through 1946. Oskar Homolka played Uncle Chris (as he did in the film), and a young man named Marlon Brando made his stage debut as Nels. Interestingly, the producers of that long-running play were Richard Rodgers and Oscar Hammerstein, and it is reasonable to assume that R&H bookmarked the play for later use as a musical.

In fact, the essential good-heartedness of the material made the play an obvious vehicle for Oscar Hammerstein, but it had to wait its turn, and by the time it worked its way up in the queue, Hammerstein was dead. Rodgers chose Martin Charnin as his lyricist, and, while Charnin is capable (*Annie*), he is no Hammerstein, and the lyrics are serviceable but not inspired. (Rodgers might have done better flying solo; his lyrics for *No Strings* are highly professional. In fact, they are sometimes brilliant.)

The musical opened in 1979, but the recording was made six years later. Liv Ullmann, the stage Mama, is replaced in the recording by Sally Ann Howes, a definite upgrade, and George Hearn and George Irving reprise their stage roles.

It is tempting to think that if the golden-voiced Howes had played Mama in the stage musical, it might have run much longer than 108 performances, but that's not fair. Ullmann is a fine actress, and the score is not musically demanding. More likely, the New York audiences just didn't respond to the old-world values of the piece the way their parents did 30-plus years before.

The music, while not vintage Rodgers, is very good. In a few cases it showcases the composer's melodic genius. A song called "When?" (dropped from the show but restored in the CD) is solid gold, and one wonders how a man can write melodies for 50 years and still be capable of surprising you. "Time" is the perfect song to sing at your daughter's wedding reception. ("How wonderful it's been to watch you grow – Time, time, time, time - time to let go.") The big love duet is "You Could Not Please Me More," and it is the quintessential Richard Rodgers ballad.

The CD is definitely worth adding to your collection, if you collect such things. I wish the program notes were more informative, but the music, the orchestrations, and the technical quality are all first-rate.

A footnote: The other night I watched a video called *Show Business*, a documentary about the making of four Broadway musicals that opened a few years ago: *Avenue Q, Wicked, Taboo*, and *Caroline, or Change*. Musicals such as these make *I Remember Mama* sound awfully good.

That's Entertainment?

T he *Times* tells us that a new Kander-Ebb musical is in the works. Ordinarily this would be a cause for celebration, and not just because Fred Ebb died a couple of years ago and anything in his trunk is worth preserving. This will be the second Fred Ebb musical to be staged posthumously, the first being *Curtains*, a clever play-in-a-play having to do with a stage-struck police detective called in to investigate a murder committed during a musical's Boston tryout run. John Kander's music was, as usual, very good, and the Ebb lyrics stylish. I didn't see the show, but I have listened to the CD often enough to remain convinced that Kander and Ebb belong right up there with the other great collaborators of Broadway's Golden Age.

The new Kander and Ebb musical is called *The Scottsboro Boys*, after the defendants in a gang-rape trial that took place in Alabama in 1931. Let us pause a second to recognize that Kander and Ebb's two blockbuster hits, *Chicago* and *Cabaret*, dealt with offbeat subjects, though in a definitely musical-comedy format. And let us acknowledge that great musicals like *Les Miz* and *Miss Saigon* can deal artistically with profound subjects. *Ragtime* dealt with racial tensions, and *No Strings* and *Kwamina* had black-white romances. Still – a musical with a gang-rape trial at its core? I have no doubt that the score will be good, but I wonder.

You may offer *Sweeney Todd* as a successful (sort of) example of depravity glorified, but Sondheim deserves to be placed in his own category. Sondheim plays are unhappy plays, maybe because Sondheim thinks that life is unhappy, and he is simply being true to life. Even when the composer gives us a good, look-on-the-bright-side song, it is sung as pastiche (see *Follies*). But the real Sondheim comes through in his *Assassins*, which invites us to listen to Lee Harvey Oswald and other assassins explain themselves. Sondheim is an enigma. The man was "adopted" as a youth by Oscar Hammerstein, whose musicals are filled to the brim with hope (walk on, walk on), June bustin' out all over, a hundred and one pounds of fun, and a hundred million miracles – none of which seems to have influenced young Stevie.

Forget all that, some people say. Hammerstein was a realist, who wrote about miscegenation (*Showboat*), racial prejudice (*South Pacific*), and other themes that were ground-breaking in their day. Granted. But Hammerstein the ground-breaker was a man not capable of writing a Sweeney Todd. Hammerstein had exquisite taste, which his protégé lacks. One guesses that Sondheim would throw up at the mere mention of taste.

The problem I have with the whole ground-breaking line is that it treats what came before as too silly for words. We hear, endlessly, that no show before *Oklahoma!* ever began with a lone cowboy on a stage, singing about a beautiful morning. Before that, we are told, musicals began with (if you can believe it) chorus lines of beautiful girls. And the plots were not credible. The shows of the 30s, shows like *Anything Goes* and *Girl Crazy* and *The Boys From Syracuse*, had one thing on their producers' minds – entertaining the audiences. How lowbrow can you get?

Look, I loved *Les Miz* and *Evita*. But I also loved *42d Street* and *Do Re Mi* and *Little Me* and *She Loves Me*, none of which had a message but all of which gave their audiences a wonderful two and a half hours.

One of my favorite movies is Preston Sturges's *Sullivan's Travels*. In it Sullivan is a successful Hollywood director of slapstick comedies who now wants to move beyond all that to direct an Important Film, which will be called *O Brother Where Art Thou?* So he takes off on an odyssey to sample the life of the oppressed masses, about which he will then write. But on his voyage he discovers that the best thing he can do for the masses is to keep making the kind of silly movies that make people laugh.

"There's a lot to be said for making people laugh in this cockamamie world," Sullivan says at the end. And, I might add, for musicals that lift your heart and set your toes tapping - and that leave the messages for Western Union and gang rape for Fox News.

Chess, The Musical

One night in early 1986 I found myself in London's West End, looking for good theater. A marquee announced a musical called *Chess*, and I, a musical theater fan and a chess player of sorts, was hooked. A review posted in the lobby gushed that one of the show's songs, "I Know Him So Well," was one of the finest book songs the reviewer had ever heard. That hooked me.

The show was – I strain to be kind here – passable. The setting was a world chess championship, the protagonists the current title holder, an obnoxious American, and the challenger, a Russian. You have to bear in mind (1) that the Cold War was in full flower in the 80s and (2) that the memory of the famous championship match between Boris Spassky and Bobby Fischer was still fresh. The political overtones heightened the drama of that match (which Fischer won) and cried out for a theatrical treatment.

Tim Rice, who had collaborated with Andrew Lloyd-Webber to give the world *Evita*, tried to talk the composer into a project based on a chess championship match between an American and a Russian, but Lloyd-Webber was deep into other projects at the time, and passed. Rice then (in 1981) joined with half of the (then dissolving) ABBA team, Benny Andersson and Bjorn Ulvaeus, and a musical called *Chess* started taking shape.

The problem, as I remember it, was a clumsy book and an inadequate score. The staging was another minus. The stage was dominated by a large chessboard, tilted at an angle, which managed to upstage the actors. Only two songs were memorable: "One Night in Bangkok" and "I Know Him So Well." Rice should have waited until Lloyd-Webber's calendar was free.

The show ran in London for three years, but was still a financial and critical failure. Still, the basic idea was okay, and Rice sat down to rewrite in preparation for taking *Chess* to Broadway. One good song ("Someone Else's Story") was added, and the character of the American was softened. The massively rewritten *Chess* opened in New York in April 1988 – and died 68 performances later, losing millions.

So why am I telling you about such an all-out floperoo? Because it has resurfaced again, this time as a so-called concert version, staged at London's Royal Albert Hall and available to Americans on DVD. And it is very good.

First, don't let the words "concert version" fool you. This is a huge production, with a philharmonic orchestra, a large chorus, dancers, and rear projections to suggest Italy (Act 1) and Thailand (Act 2). The cast is topnotch, notably Josh Groban as the Russian and Adam Pascal as the American. The music has been greatly improved over the years, or maybe the original was better than it sounded; that orchestra and chorus may have made the difference.

Rice hasn't forgotten the touches that made *Evita* so riveting. Who can forget the tableau of the Buenos Aires upper class, gliding en masse from one side of the stage to the other while denouncing Peron's mistress? In *Chess*, a group of "old boys" at the British embassy cluck their displeasure at all the asylum-seekers cluttering up their offices. And a character called "The Arbiter" serves the same purpose as does Che in *Evita*.

Some plotting weaknesses still show, especially in Act 2, and the song "Someone Else's Story" is inexplicably given to the Russian's wife rather than to his girlfriend. But these flaws are outweighed by the effect of what is, over-all, a dazzling production.

Rice is rumored to be planning another go at Broadway, but a *Chess* on the scale of the Royal Albert concert would be financially impossible in New York. My suggestion is to grab the DVD, because *Chess* will never be this good again.

Wegmans....The Musical

I was one of 900-plus people lucky enough to squeeze into the auditorium of the Algonquin Regional High School in Northborough, MA the other night. The occasion was a performance of *Wegmans...The Musical*. The production, staged by Algonquin's Advanced Drama Class, began as a 20-minute skit, but the class kept hanging subplots and musical ideas on the tree until it blossomed into a full, two-act musical. The concept was inspired, and the execution was terrific.

If you've never heard of Wegmans, it's a chain of grandiose grocery stores in the northeast, and its first venture into New England was the Northborough store, which opened last fall. The Northborough Wegmans is as innovative as it is huge – so innovative that a battalion of Russians, armed with cameras and notebooks, descended on Northborough to capture the store's essence, with an intent to clone it in Moscow. (Good luck with that.) Words can hardly describe the Wegmans experience, but a hurricane has just hit the New England grocery scene.

The story of *Wegmans....The Musical* pivots around twin brothers. Teddy manages Wegmans, and his bother runs a competitor, Acme Foods. Teddy is all good, and Roy is all bad - and determined to rain on Teddy's parade. Roy hires a young clerk, Sheldon, and convinces him that his destiny is to become a Jason Bourne and save the world from the evils of Wegmans. So Sheldon takes a job at

Wegmans and tries to dig up dirt on Wegmans and its manager. There are enough subplots to keep the cast of 18 busy. There are a couple of romances and there is a senile old man who is determined to walk to Wegmans with his walker (think of a shuffling Tim Conway). It's all over the top, but once you accept that, it's hilarious.

The music is "imported" from *Les Miz, West Side Story, Rent, Fiddler*, and other Broadway hits, with situational lyrics grafted onto the familiar tunes. Examples: Act One closes with a parody of the barricade scene from Les Miz, with the faux marching and, in place of the tricolor, a waving Massachusetts state flag, all to lyrics that celebrate "One Great Store." And the show opens with "Seasons of Love" from *Rent* translated into "Wegmans We Love" ("525,600 square feet").

Only two members of the cast could really sing: Steve Tzanibos (Teddy) and Juliana Fiore (a Wegmans worker). But the entire cast could act, which is what you'd expect from an Advanced Drama Class, and the enraptured audience helped create a sense of jubilation. Among the enraptured were representatives of Wegmans, and a video record will surely find its way to Wegmans' Rochester, NY headquarters.

So hats off to Maura Morrison's Advanced Drama Class at Algonquin (known to its students as "the Gonk.") They showed great enterprise, imagination, and talent in pulling this together.

Monarch of the Glen

In 1999, the BBC launched a weekly television series called *Monarch of the Glen*, based very loosely on some novels written by Compton MacKenzie. The series was wildly successful, not only in Britain, but on the European continent, in Australia and New Zealand, and, via PBS, in the United States. It ran for seven seasons, has been rerun since, and the BBC does a brisk business in DVDs. It has also spawned a cult of followers, who call themselves "boglies." (The series takes place at a Scottish estate called Glenbogle.)

Two old pros anchor the series: Richard Briers plays Hector MacDonald, the Laird of Glenbogle, and Susan Hampshire plays his wife Molly. As the series begins, their son, Archie, is preparing to open an upscale restaurant in London when he hears that his father, Hector, has had an accident "in the loch." Archie drops everything to catch the sleeper to Scotland and Glenbogle. There he finds his father just fine after his dunking, and Hector and Molly seize the moment to inform Archie that, for tax reasons, they have made him the new laird of the 40,000-acre, near-bankrupt estate.

Archie wants none of this, but events conspire to keep him at Glenbogle, where he tries to right the sinking ship while romancing the local teacher, his old girlfriend up from London, and Glenbogle's chief cook and housekeeper. The acting is superb, the writing even better, and the scenery spectacular. (The fictional

Glenbogle is actually a highland estate called Ardverikie, to which boglies make regular pilgrimages.)

What accounts for the extraordinary worldwide response to *Monarch of the Glen*? First, there is that writing, always wise and witty. Second, Briers and Hampshire are joined by a flock of fine young actors from the BBC's seemingly limitless pool. Third, it is clean as a daisy – no sex, no foul language, no violence. (But the series is not *Mary Poppins*; much of it would be over the heads of small children.)

Seven seasons is an eternity in television, and actors must be written out of the story line when contracts expire or better opportunities call them away. (Richard Briers, after three seasons, left to spend more time with his grandchildren.) The writers coped with these comings and goings fairly well, but whenever a central character is dropped from the story, there is a palpable feeling of loss, which says something about the program's hold on its audience.

The first four of the seven series are now available on DVDs rentable from Netflix. Many boglies have bought DVDs of the final series from the UK, sometimes buying multi-region DVD players expressly for the purpose. You will also find a bustling trade in *Monarch of the Glen* DVDs on eBay.

More Lost Treasures

In the 1980s, PBS and A&E aired a number of choice British plays, some of which I videotaped for posterity – and against the time when I might live in the boonies and not have easy access to quality entertainment. Well, I now live in the boonies, sort of, and I have well over 100 cable TV channels, plus Netflix, plus an active amateur theater community nearby. But I am still glad I taped those plays, because none of them is now available commercially – no DVD, no videotape, no Netflix, and no longer shown by the TV channels, which seem to be preoccupied with dross.

But back to these tapes. There are five of them in my collection, and they are all keepers.

Quartermaine's Terms

This one, written by Simon Gray, is the best of the lot. It takes place mostly in the teachers' lounge at a British school chartered to teach the English language and culture to foreigners. The teachers are all fascinating characters, and we get to know them, their families (by reference), and their problems very well.

There is the classics teacher Henry, who boasts incessantly about his daughter, studying for her "0-level" exams. There is the spinster Melanie, who regrets rejecting Henry years ago and now cares for her invalid mother, whom she despises. There is Derek, newly employed as a part-timer, who is an accident-prone sad sack. There is Mark, an aspiring novelist whose wife has just left him. There is Anita, a pregnant woman maintaining a brave front in the face of her husband's affairs. And then there is St. John ("Sinjin" in Britspeak) Quartermaine, an amiable, chronically forgetful fellow, everybody's friend but an incompetent teacher, barely tolerated by the principal, Eddie, played brilliantly by John Gielgud. Edward Fox gives the performance of his life as Quartermaine, Eleanor Bron is the unhappy Melanie, Peter Jeffrey is an unforgettable Henry, and every other cast member is absolutely perfect.

Simon Gray has referred to his play as a "serious comedy," and that about nails it. Certainly I know of no play in which the characters' personalities are so fully revealed in the space of less than two hours. It is, simply, a dramatic masterpiece, and it is a crime against humanity that the BBC production appears to be lost forever.

Relatively Speaking

This is the farce that established Alan Ayckbourn as Britain's preeminent contemporary playwright. Young Greg and Ginny have been living together for about a month in a London flat. Greg loves Ginny but is uncomfortable knowing that at least one man previously shared the apartment and the bed with Ginny. A constant stream of gifts (chocolates, flowers) and a pair of men's slippers found under the bed don't help.

When Ginny announces that she is off for a weekend to visit her parents in the suburbs, Greg snatches what he believes to be the parents' address and sets out by train to meet them himself and to declare his intentions. But the address is not that of Ginny's parents, but that of Ginny's old flame Philip, a middle-aged man leading a sedate life with his wife Sheila, whom he also suspects of having a secret liaison.

Greg enters the garden to find Sheila at breakfast, and the mistaken-identity plot is launched. Greg believes Philip and Sheila to be Ginny's parents, Philip believes Greg is Sheila's paramour, and Sheila doesn't know what to think. When Ginny shows up (her intention was to make a final break from Philip), the farce turns uproarious. The far-fetched plot demands pitch-perfect performances by the actors, and it gets them. Nigel Hawthorne is Philip, Gwen Watford his dotty wife, Michael Maloney is Greg, and Ginny is played by a yummy, mini-skirted Imogen Stubbs. The four are the only characters in the play, and the two sets are simple, so the play is revived often. But this production is still the gold standard, and, since my videotape is giving out, I would be ecstatic if someone would produce a DVD.

Waters of the Moon

This play, by N.C. Hunter, was shown as part of an A&E series called "Stage" in 1983. The setting is a stately old guest house in Devonshire, inhabited by four permanent residents living out their twilight years in quiet boredom.

There are two elderly ladies, one irrepressively jolly, the other melancholy and self-pitying, a retired Army colonel, and a courtly Austrian exile, trying to adapt to English life and customs. Other characters include the housekeeper, Mrs. Daly, and her two children, a young man afflicted with "a weak chest" and a 28-year-old daughter embittered by what she sees as a dead-end life.

A heavy snowstorm howls outside, and there is a knocking at the door. Then into this sleepy environment blow the Lancasters, an upper-class British couple and their daughter, Their car is stuck in the snow, and they require shelter. The woman, played brilliantly by Penelope Keith (BBC mainstay Geoffrey Palmer plays her husband), imperiously takes over the house, its guests, the Dalys, and the play. Like "Quartermaine's Terms," this one classifies as a serious comedy, with the accent on the "serious." My tape is now a quarter-century old and starting to look a bit tired. But the content is so good that one can put up with the technical imperfections.

Season's Greetings

Another "serious comedy" by Alan Ayckbourn, with Geoffrey Palmer (who must be the most steadily employed actor in history), Barbara Flynn (who is still going strong), Peter Vaughan, Anna Massey, and other old BBC friends, all getting together for a Christmas holiday. Palmer is busy preparing his annual puppet show for the children (dreaded by children and grown-ups alike), Vaughan is a right-wing zealot ready for whatever the new order throws at him, and Massey is a spinsterly mass of neuroses ready to take the plunge (or is she?) with a new writer friend. It's all impossibly complicated, and before the farce ends the writer is shot (Vaughan thinks he's a burglar), Palmer, an impossibly incompetent doctor, wrongly calls him dead, and Massey's virginity is not an issue after all (the writer is more interested in Flynn). Well, you had to be there.

Hotel Du Lac

This one is actually available as a DVD, but it is a Region 2 DVD (for European DVD players only), and most Americans are to be deprived of this excellent production of the Anita Brookner novel, starring Anna Massey, Denholm Elliott, and a sterling supporting cast, notably including a wonderful Googie Withers. Massey plays an English novelist who leaves her intended (but unwanted) husband at the altar and escapes the ensuing shame by fleeing to Switzerland, where she puts up at the Hotel Du Lac, a posh lakeside retreat where she encounters several (mostly British) vacationers, including a wealthy widow (Withers) and her pampered daughter, a single woman (Patricia Hodge) bored with life and starved for companionship, and a successful electronics executive (Elliott) who attempts to sell Massey on the idea of a marriage of convenience. Most novels suffer from the compression into a two-hour TV production, but this one does not. The essential wisdom of the book comes through here, and I can't think of a thing of real value that the telescript could have added.

There are undoubtedly many other television productions of excellent British plays that were shipped across the Atlantic in the 70s and 80s for a brief shining moment on American TV – and then seen no more. How can it be that now, when there are hundreds of channels for the asking, there is no place to find them?

2000 Acres of Sky

The British are the masters of the miniseries. The Americans may be the masters of musical theater and fast food, but when it comes to miniseries we aren't even close. The Masterpiece Theater franchise alone gives them the cup, but then there are also the likes of *Brideshead Revisited* and *Monarch of the Glen* and *Traffik* and *Ballykissangel* and countless others. The British seem to have an unlimited supply of good writers (many of them long dead) and an unlimited supply of (live) leading men, leading women, and character actors, all of whom seem to have flawless diction and experience with the Royal Shakespeare Company or the Old Vic.

Every viewer seems to have his or her favorite in the miniseries treasure chest. One believes there will never be another *Upstairs, Downstairs*, another prefers *Tinker,*

Tailor, while a third votes for *Foyle's War*. My own favorites are all the aforementioned, plus one newcomer, whose praises I now wish to sing.

The series is called *2000 Acres of Sky*, and if this produces a sea of blank stares it is not surprising. The series, produced in Scotland, has never made it across the Atlantic. Never, in any form. No DVD formatted for U.S. television, no Netflix, no PBS airing. That's a crime, because this is one compelling drama, with intelligent writing and some of the most fascinating characters and plot turns you'll ever see, all played against that awesome Hebridean scenery.

Here's the situation that launches the series: On the fictional island of Ronansay the small community faces a crisis, as the school population has dropped to three – two fewer than the minimum required by the Scottish school authority. If the school closes, as seems likely, the three remaining students face a long ferry ride to and from another island. Worse, their parents will probably leave the island, driving one more stake into the heart of the island as it fights for survival.

The solution, Ronansay's people decide, lies in attracting a family with at least two children. What the island can offer the family is an abandoned B&B and help in making a livelihood on an island that is quite beautiful and attracts a fair number of tourists. So they run an ad in the British papers.

To Abby Wallace, a mother of two small children, living in noisy, crime-ridden East London, the ad's prospect of a better life for her and her children seems irresistible. The catch: Abby's husband abandoned her and her children years before. The ad says Ronansay is looking for a married couple with children, and Abby is a single Mom. But living down the corridor in the tenement is Kenny, a buddy of Abby's – nothing more – whose ambition, to the extent he has any, is to be a rock star. Kenny will never make it, because he doesn't have the talent, but he is a close enough pal (who loves to tell Abby's children outrageous bedtime stories) so that Abby asks him to join her in answering the ad and sending a staged photo of "the family."

What happens if Ronansay chooses them from all the applicants? We can sort that out later, says Abby, implying that once the children are installed in the school, Kenny can safely return to London and his gigs.

The starting premise is obviously promising, and before long we meet and come to know the characters that make life on Ronansay miniseries-worthy. But it is the development of the character Kenny that makes this series so worth watching. Writer Timothy Prager (who wrote 21 out of the 22 episodes) transforms Kenny the born loser, with his freaky face and crucifix earring, into Kenny the magnetic centerpiece of the drama. Kenny, played to perfection by Paul Kaye, is forever wondering what his purpose in life is, and we wonder too, while we become captivated by his essential goodness.

The series played in the U.K from 2001 through 2003, and it won its share of critical praise and awards. Its failure (so far) to find an American outlet may have something to do with those Scottish accents, though captions are available. (*Monarch of the Glen* was also filmed in Scotland, but most of its principal actors spoke BBC English.)

You could write a book about the cultural differences that consign most British miniseries to PBS, while commercial TV gives us The Sopranos and Desperate Housewives.

P.S. You can buy Region 2 DVDs of this series from dealers in the UK, and you can play these on "multi-region" DVD players. (Ask at the store.)

A Carousel for the Ages

L ate in April, PBS broadcast a concert version of the Rodgers and Hammerstein musical *Carousel*. I have seen several productions of *Carousel* and, like many, I regard it as Rodgers's finest score and Hammerstein's most soaring poetry. But I have never heard a *Carousel* so musically rich or so well sung as this one. For those who treasure music rather than stagecraft it will stand as the definitive *Carousel* for a long time.

First, the leads. Nathan Gunn is Billy Bigelow, the rough-edged carousel barker. Gunn has one of the strongest, truest voices in the world of opera, and he is equally at home in musical theater. (He is also in the cast in the CD of another Rodgers & Hammerstein musical, *Allegro*.) His "Soliloquy" is on a par with John Raitt's, which is saying a lot, and his duet with Julie, "If I Loved You," is riveting.

Kelli O'Hara is perfection as Julie Jordan. In fact, whenever I think of *Carousel* in the future, I will conjure up a mental picture of Kelli O'Hara. The make-up crew and wigmaker deserve a special award, so absolutely *right* does she look – and act, with beautifully expressive eyes revealing a deep love for the caddish Billy. I should add that I have never heard Kelli O'Hara sing as well as she does here.

Since in this play the music is the thing, it is clear that *Carousel* deserves nothing less than the New York Philharmonic. To play that overture with a pit orchestra should be a mortal sin. This orchestra, with Rob Fisher conducting, is heaven to listen to.

The supporting cast is fine. Opera's Stephanie Blythe as Julie's cousin Netty sings "June is Busting Out All Over" with good-hearted gusto and leads the chorus in the anthem "You'll Never Walk Alone." Enoch Snow and Carrie Pipperidge are played by Jason Danieley and Jessie Mueller, and while neither is at home with the comedic business one associates with these characters, both are in fine voice. Kate Burton makes the most of her small but key role as carousel owner Mrs. Mullen, and Shuler Hensley handles the difficult role of Jigger, Billy's partner in crime, perfectly. It's not easy to play a bad guy and a comic character simultaneously, but Shuler pulls it off – and sings well, too. And John Cullum must be just the kind of star-keeper Oscar Hammerstein had in mind when he wrote the final scenes.

As you probably know, the plot of *Carousel* is derived from Molnar's *Liliom*. Rodgers and Hammerstein made major plot alterations, but Molnar deserves credit; without his approval, we would be deprived of what *Time* called the greatest musical of the twentieth century.

The staging is arranged so that the ensemble comes and goes through the same space that the orchestra inhabits, a device that somehow forces one to remain aware of the wonderful Don Walker arrangements and the artistry of the Philharmonic.

All told, this is the finest theatrical production in the Live at Lincoln Center series I have ever seen, and we are indebted to those who made it possible.

Bloomer Girl, Dearest Enemy

S anta, who knows my passions, gave me two videos that I cherish. One is the Rodgers & Hart musical *Dearest Enemy*, the other is *Bloomer Girl*, written by Harold Arlen and E.Y. Harburg. Both shows were television productions, in 1955 and 1956. They are black and white videos, and the technical quality is, well, primitive. But the material! Let me tell you about them.

Both are set against the definitive wars of our country. The American Revolution supplies the plot for *Dearest Enemy*, which opened in 1925, just months after the Rodgers & Hart breakthrough review, *The Garrick Gaieties*. *Dearest Enemy* was thus the first book musical written by the pair of youngsters. (Rodgers was only 23.) The story line: General Howe and his contingent of British soldiers are bent on capturing George Washington, who is planning to rendezvous with one of his officers. The British are staying at the New York inn of Mrs. Murray, and Mrs. Murray and the other women at the inn contrive to detain the British long enough to spoil their plan.

The romantic leads are played by Robert Sterling (a British officer) and Anne Jeffreys (one of the American contrivers). The comic relief is furnished by two old pros, Cyril Ritchard as General Howe and Cornelia Otis Skinner as Mrs. Murray. Only one song had lasting popularity: *Here in My Arms*. *Here's a Kiss* gave a hint of the melodic treasures that Rodgers would give us over the decades to come, and *Cheerio* and *Sweet Peter* (Stuyvesant) were good novelty songs. The show was telecast (live, of course) on November 26, 1955. The credits include co-scripter Neil Simon and producer Max Liebman, best remembered today (by those old enough) as the creator of *Your Show of Shows.*

The other video, *Bloomer Girl,* is one of the great musicals of the 40s. Composer Harold Arlen and lyricist "Yip" Harburg had teamed up five years earlier to give the world the score for *The Wizard of Oz,* and the two outdid themselves in *Bloomer Girl,* with one excellent song after another, including *Evelina, The Eagle and Me, Right as the Rain, When the Boys Come Home,* and *Sunday at Cicero Falls* (with the memorable line "virtue is its own revenge"). The television cast is top-drawer, headed by Barbara Cook (pre-Marian the Librarian, pre-Cunegonde), with Keith Andes, Carmen Mathews, and Paul Ford providing strong support. Agnes DeMille staged the dances, and four of the dancers were in the original cast in 1944. (The television production was aired on May 28, 1956.) The title refers to the women's campaign to replace hoop skirts with bloomers, but the weightier theme is the country's schism over slavery. Harburg, always an ardent liberal, wrote one of his best lyrics for *The Eagle and Me*. ("What makes the gopher leave its hole, trembling with fear and fright? Maybe the gopher's got a soul, wanting to see the light...") This is a more serious play than *Dearest Enemy,* but it is still a musical *comedy*. There is a war in the wings in both plays, but not a drop of blood is spilled in either.

Any lover of musicals will value the chance to see these telecasts – the only surviving record of either play. It is hard to understand how Arthur Freed let *Bloomer Girl* escape the MGM treatment.

When watching these grainy kinescopes, it is easy to cluck at the their technical shortcomings. But wait. Viewers in 1955 and 1956 may not have had Blue Ray or Surround Sound, but they could watch good studio productions of important musicals. What do we have in their place? Two and a Half Men? CSI? People 50 years ago could watch good variety shows, with Jackie Gleason, Sid Caesar, Carol Burnett. They had The Bell Telephone Hour, Playhouse 90, Studio One. We have big, flat screens – and very little of quality on them.

Page Eight

David Hare, who has been writing screenplays for a long time, has polished off a corker of a spy story, called *Page Eight*. And it is timely, in the light of recent revelations that the American spooks at the NSA have been eavesdropping on the European spooks. The movie, which was directed as well as written by Hare, benefits from a first-class cast, headed by Bill Nighy, who plays MI-5 analyst Johnny Worricker with his usual laconic persona – a perfect fit for this character. Also in the cast are Michael Gambon, who plays MI-5's Director General and Worricker's mentor, and Ralph Fiennes, who plays the British Prime

Minister. It will not spoil things if I tell you that the plot pivots on whether the PM knew about the Americans' rendition of prisoners to countries known to tolerate torture.

Most of the male characters, especially Worricker and his boss, are decent human beings, while the lead baddy (apart from the PM) is a female - Judy Davis, who is terrific as Jill Tankard, a colleague of Worricker's at MI-5. The dialog is crisp, a Hare staple, and the production values are good. In fact, one wonders why more wasn't made of the film when it was released in 2011. Maybe Nighy wasn't big enough a star to warrant major promotion; if Johnny Depp or George Clooney had played the lead there might have been more, but it wouldn't have been nearly as good a movie.

As mentioned, there are several references to the sharing or nonsharing of intelligence between the American and British intelligence agencies, and Hare makes no bones about the realities of the situation. Intelligence people lie – that's what they do, even to each other – and to think otherwise is plain foolish. If Barack Obama summons the head of the CIA or NSA and asks him a straight question, will he get a truthful answer? Maybe, but one would be foolish to bet one's life on it. The same is true the world over.

Sharing top billing with Nighy, for reasons unknown to me, is Rachel Weisz, who plays Nancy Pierpan, a neighbor of Worricker's. She is the nearest thing to a romantic element the film offers, and her character adds little to the plot. In fact, the pace quickens in the scenes at the offices of MI-5 and reaches a crescendo in the scene between Worricker and the Prime Minister.

Good spy dramas don't need shootings or stabbings to keep you on the edge of your seat. What they need is believable characters who talk intelligently about subjects that matter. It helps if the central character is sympathetic and perceived to be in mortal danger. *Page Eight* delivers on all counts.

Hobson's Choice (The Ballet)

*H*obson's Choice is chiefly remembered today as a very good old (1954) movie starring Charles Laughton. But there is also a ballet based on the same turn-of the-century play, and if you like ballet – if even if you don't – you might seek it out. It will open your eyes and ears.

The ballet is by David Bintley, and the music was composed by Paul Reade. The only performance that was recorded, as far as I know, is by the Birmingham Royal Ballet Company in 1992, and I believe it is available. (I taped it when it was broadcast on Bravo a long time ago.)

The story: Hobson, a bootmaker, has three daughters who run the shop under their father's iron hand. Hobson is irresponsible and an alcoholic, and the shop survives only through the hard work of the bootmaker Will Mossop, who labors unseen and unrewarded. Hobson dominates his daughters, for whom marriage is out of the question. But the oldest daughter, Maggie, has an independent streak, as well as an eye for Will Mossop. I will reveal no more, other than to say that the story ends happily.

The principal dancers are Michael O'Hare (Will Mossop) and Karen Donovan (Maggie), and they are excellent. Hobson is played by Desmond Kelly, a veteran dancer who is also the production's ballet master.

The music is beautiful. Composer Reade has chosen to interpolate an old song, *Lily of Laguna*, which adds greatly to a pivotal scene. The orchestrations make full use of the large Royal Ballet Orchestra; in fact, the audio quality of the recording exceeds the video quality – a reflection of the state of technology in 1992.

I know next to nothing about ballet, but I know what I like, and I like David Bintley's ballet very much. If you're interested, you can sample a bit of it by searching YouTube

The Sound of (Live) Music

It has been four days since NBC presented a live performance of *The Sound of Music*, time enough for all the critics to lambast Carrie Underwood because she isn't Julie Andrews and to lament the play's cloying sentimentality. Enough, already. Someone should speak up for the production, which, despite a few shortcomings, was a high-quality rendition of a high-quality musical. And Carrie Underwood should hold her head high; she was an excellent Maria. As a matter of fact, hearing that the network was planning to air a *live* performance, I sensed a disaster in the wings, but I needn't have worried. NBC pulled it off with flying colors.

First, the material: This *Sound of Music* was based not on the movie, which everybody has seen, but on the Broadway musical, which relatively few people now alive have seen. That play opened on November 16, 1959, ran for 1433 performances, and won mostly rave reviews, especially for Mary Martin, its star. (Theodore Bikel was the baron.) At least two of the songs were not used in the 1965 blockbuster movie: but were fortunately resurrected for the NBC production: "No Way to Stop It" and "How Can Love Survive?" For the broadcast, the producers also decided to use one song written specially for the movie: the lovely "Something Good."

As I said, most critics loved the play. Frank Aston of the World-Telegram called it "The loveliest musical imaginable," and Richard Watts of the Post wrote that the "show has a warm-hearted, unashamedly sentimental, and strangely gentle charm that is wonderfully endearing." The raves are worth noting, because the movie, so beloved by the public, has become a favorite piñata of some critics, who routinely savage its sentimentality (*The Sound of Mucus*).

The cast: It was up to Carrie Underwood to carry the production, just as it was up to Mary Martin and Julie Andrews, and Ms Underwood did far better than one could reasonably expect, given her limited dramatic experience. She *looked* right, and that alone put her on second base. Add a fine voice, and that put her on third. There was not a flat note (none that I could detect, anyway) and not a jarring line or reaction. No, she's not Julie Andrews (who is?), but remember that if Julie flubbed a line or didn't hit a note right, why, they simply shot it over, as many times as necessary, until it was perfect. As for Mary Martin, she was 46 (!) when she played Maria, and she had *decades* of stage experience behind her.

The supporting cast was excellent, notably including Laura Benanti as Elsa Schrader. Laura is a legitimate singer and played the role with warmth and wit. (Eleanor Parker, the movie's Frau Schrader, was edgier and did no singing.) Christian Borle was a solid Max Detweiler (the impresario), particularly when singing with Laura Benanti, and the children were adorable – and good singers, to boot. If there was a weak link it was the baron. Stephen Moyer was stiff and sang poorly. He looked the part, and that must have landed him the job. But that only got him to second base, where, alas, he died. Audra McDonald, as the Mother Superior, was formidable, as she always is.

The interior sets were well executed. As for the exteriors (the Austrian Alps), they were embarrassingly phony, although I don't know how they could have finessed that except by bringing in a video of the real Alps or resorting to computer graphics – both of which would have brought howls from viewers who were promised a *live* production. In 1959, faux mountains probably didn't matter, but expectations have been inflated since then.

Carrie Underwood is 30 now – the same age Julie Andrews was when she made The Movie. Let's hope Carrie's career has the same kind of arc that Julie's had. And let's hope that NBC doesn't let the naysayers keep it from televising more live musicals.

Sharing the Journey

I should begin these reflections by repaying a debt: Aside from my hard-working parents, the greatest influences on my life were the Jesuits who shepherded me through high school. To quote Frederic March in *The Bridges at Toko-Ri*, "Where do we get such men?" And I echo March, thinking of the men who were giving their lives to us at B.C. High. Where did we get such men?

Sixty-three years ago I graduated from college, wondering what I was going to do with the rest of my life. I had majored in English and contributed poems to the local newspaper and some drawings and some fiction to the college literary magazine. I had acted in a lot of plays in school and in community theater, and it was widely (and wrongly) assumed that I planned to make the stage my career.

In the early fifties job-seeking was a hit-or-miss proposition. The competition, older and wiser (WW2 veterans were everywhere), left little for people like me. So I taught high-school algebra for a year and, as a National Guard officer, signed up for a short tour of active duty in order to attend classes in radar. Parlaying all this into a résumé, I applied for and was offered a position with an engineering firm as a technical writer. The alternative was a job with a firm that sold stamps and catalogs to retail outlets. I would have supervised a roomful of young ladies who sorted stamps and packaged them for sale at Woolworth's. The technical-writing job paid ten dollars a week more, so I took it.

That decision set me on a course that took me into the technology explosion of the second half of the twentieth century. Eventually I was deeply involved in the semiconductor revolution – integrated circuits, microprocessors, Silicon Valley, and the rest. There was excitement, growth, world travel, and a good life for my family. All because of an extra ten dollars a week.

Though I was enmeshed in technology, I never lost my appetite for books, theater, music, and the arts. I have often wondered whether my split personality was due to the genes I inherited from my father (a Dutchman, with an affinity for math) and my mother (an Irish immigrant, with a love of music and theater). Anyway, by the time I retired, I had amassed a good library of books, DVDs, CDs, videotapes, and sheet music.

Looking back, it all turned out pretty well, though I sometimes wonder about the roads I didn't take. I probably could have earned a living in theater, though probably as a writer, not an actor. As for the stamp job, I'm pretty sure it would have been a disaster. One thing I know: The arts – good books, beautiful music, rich theater (especially, for me, musical theater) – these are the things that help make life worth the trip. At the top of the list, of course, is family, and in that department I won the lottery.

The Final Cut

Of course, like all trips, a journey through the arts is much better if it's shared. That, dear reader, is what drove me to compile this book. Along the way, I have had such traveling companions as Oscar Hammerstein, Richard Rodgers, Jerome Kern, Evelyn Waugh, and Anthony Trollope. And now you have shared some of the experience.